A Subaltern in Serbia

A Subaltern in Serbia

With the Tenth (Irish) Division in the Balkans
During the First World War

ILLUSTRATED

A. Donovan Young

LEONAUR

A Subaltern in Serbia
With the Tenth (Irish) Division in the Balkans During the First World War
by A. Donovan Young

ILLUSTRATED

First published under the title
A Subaltern in Serbia

Leonaur is an imprint of Oakpast Ltd

ISBN: 978-1-78282-940-9 (hardcover)
ISBN: 978-1-78282-941-6 (softcover)

http://www.leonaur.com

Publisher's Notes

Contents

Preface

In the minds of many, there will still linger threads of the story of how the Anglo-French attempted to go to the assistance of Serbia in the latter part of 1915, while the gallant little Serbian Army was offering so stubborn a resistance to the invading Austro-German-Bulgar Forces.

The Allies' landing at Salonika; the campaign among the snow-clad mountains of Serbia, attended by great hardships, and conducted under conditions before which the imagination pales; and the inevitable but none the less sensational collapse of the Expedition and the withdrawal into Greece of the small Allied Force, form but an insignificant chapter in the history of the war. To those who remain of the Tenth (Irish) Division, as it was then composed, it will, however, remain something more than a memory.

The brief sketch which follows is necessarily incomplete, and lays no claim to be anything but a rough chronicling of the events which attended the Expedition so far as it concerned one of the Irish Battalions which took part in that short-lived campaign in Serbia.

A. D. Y.

Macedonia, June, 1916.

CHAPTER 1

A First Glimpse of Salonika

One cloudy morning early in the month of October 1915, H. M. Auxiliary Cruiser ——— (6,000 tons) swept into Salonika Harbour with the assurance of a super-Dreadnought. She was evidently relieved when the evidence of the latest rather humiliating use to which she had been put—in the shape of 500 khaki-clad figures, dumped aboard her at Mudros, the Dardanelles Base—was finally packed away on lighters bound for the shore. And just as glad as H. M. ——— was to wash her hands of us, so were we pleased to part company with her, for, as a broad, straight-limbed Dorset youth of the draft wrote to the lady of his affections down in "Darsotshoire," it had been "terrible rough," and the holds of the late West African cargo Coaster which had suddenly leapt to the importance of an auxiliary cruiser in the British Navy, were about the most inhospitable quarters that British Tommies had ever presented a glum face at.

"I don't wish yer no 'arm", uttered a Cockney youth in my platoon, as from the lighter we took a glad farewell look at the Ex-Coaster, "but I 'opes—", and then his feelings so overcame him that "the remainder of his no doubt pleasant wish was lost in an excess of vituperation.

An hour later our draft from the Dorsetshire regiment marched with clattering step through the cobble-laid streets of Salonika with orders to report to the 10th (Irish) Division, of which the advanced details had, a few days previously, arrived from the Dardanelles.

It was not the most auspicious of days, for the rain descended in torrents before we had completed our four-mile march to the British Camp at Lembet. Here a few scattered, muddy tents broke the monotony of the huge, rain-sodden plain and marked the beginning of the British arrival on Macedonian soil. On the town side of Lembet, a French regiment of infantry, newly arrived, bustled excitedly round their khaki bivouacs.

Salonika (or Thesalonika), in October 1915, was very much more of a novelty then than this ancient Macedonian city, which is and always has been such a source of joy to the Antiquarian, became a few months later, when, almost daily, huge transports were depositing their human cargoes on Greek soil. Nobody could be quite sure that we were not, metaphorically speaking, living in the centre of a minefield, and one which was quite liable to blow us sky high, should the powers in Greece arrive at the conclusion that the Allies' "invasion" of Greek Macedonia was hardly reconcilable with the country's dignity, and might have to be forcibly discouraged.

The wavering, weak and nervous attitude had not at that time manifested itself in the ruling powers in Greece, nor was it deemed likely—or even possible—at any rate in the minds of our lay diplomats of the mess, that Greece would develop an attitude of incomprehensible weakness and eat the Allies' "humble pie" on successive occasions in the way she subsequently did. As the reader will realise, events in Greece at that period rather justified these feelings.

Away in the harbour, however, we could see over the tops of Salonika's white-washed houses and white minarets the masts of half a dozen or so British and French men-of-war the most reassuring sight that could meet the eyes of Britishers in a strange land. We knew that our friend the Greek would not readily invite a sampling of the quality of those naval guns bristling shorewards.

On the day following our arrival, the 7th (Service) Batt., of the Royal Munster Fusiliers, which we had come to reinforce, landed from the Dardanelles Base after strenuous times at Suvla.

Our first few days in Salonika might well have dampened the spirits of the most hardened soldier. Torrential rains had already

10TH IRISH DIVISION ON THE MARCH

transferred Lembet into a quagmire, and the streets of the old City ran with mud and water. A day and a night the most miserable in our then immature experience passed before our lynx-eyed quartermaster succeeded in his search for tents, and loud was the cheer when the first consignment emerged through the mist and rain. Ten days later it was amusing to read the skittish accounts in London Dailies of the luxury which surrounded the British troops in Salonika.

Need I say that the bright picture of Tommy Atkins reposing in luxurious apartments in Salonika's rather imposing hotels was one which was never realised as far as we were concerned. True, the palatial "Splendide", the most hospitable of Salonika's hotels, resounded with the clanking of spurs and was rendered bright and gorgeous by the red and gold of generals and of their polished staffs; but we, after enjoying an excellent dinner at the "Splendide," or in the luring brightness of the Olymphus Palace, had no alternative but to hie ourselves to our rain-soaked tents and our beds of soft mud.

The British forces in Salonika at that time consisted of one division—the Tenth. We were regarded with suspicious curiosity by the mixed Greco-Turkish population and with an entire absence of enthusiasm. From the first, the French were accepted with more or less a show of cordiality; the British, it seemed to us, were only tolerated from necessity. Doubtless the grasping Greek trader realised that though his pride might suffer from the "intrusion" of the Allies, his pocket decidedly would not.

Never was any difficulty experienced in purchasing whatever we required "at a price", and the price—Oh Heavens! Floca's, the Splendide, and the Olymphus Palace provided, as they do now, a tempting lunch and an excellent dinner; and the Odeon an execrable performance which a fifth-rate Music Hall in England would not dare offend its critical patrons by putting on.

And yet Salonika, in October 1915, was quite unashamed in its lack of real entertainment or resorts for a subaltern with leave for the evening; its "Hullo! Salonika!" and subsequent revues, then undreamt of, was to my mind infinitely more attractive than the Salonika of 1916. One could explore its interesting features; visit its wonderful old arch, and its antiquity shops (almost as old as the antiquities which filled the windows) without the necessity of manoeuvring one's way through the thronged streets which synchronised with the later arrival of big British and French reinforcements, and the landing of Russians, and Italians, and Serbs (from Corfu) in their thousands.

One could even wander into Steins, and cause an obviously German assistant to cast uncomfortable glances in one's direction, or cause a perceptible flutter in a rarely patronised shop whose management fondled the hope of an extensive patronage from British officers and men in future days. The Turk, in his *fez*, swarthy faced, and of sombre appearance, sat outside his grimy shop, regarding us with idle curiosity.

The Greek Highlander, in close fitting knee-breeches of white flannel, tasselled cap and pompom-toed shoes, made the most strikingly picturesque object of all, and was in striking contrast to the somewhat foppish and jaunty young Greek Civilian in his more or less continental garb. Continental and Cosmopolitan today, (1922), Salonika, as we knew it then, marked a turning point between East and West; giving an atmosphere typically Eastern one moment and as obviously Western the next.

You would meet a resplendent Greek captain of infantry, his sword clanking officiously behind him, in Venezilos street, while, around the corner, you would stumble upon a Native of the East, skilfully balancing himself on the pole of his bullock cart and calling shrilly to his bull. Or you would see a slim, dark haired and bright eyed Greek lady, dressed in the daintiest and latest Parisian fashion, trip past you, avoiding proximity with the coarse peasant girl, in her plentiful but not unpicturesque garb, who shuffles uncomfortably along the narrow pavement of Venezilos street, and heaves a sigh of relief on turning into one of the less reputable and more muddy thoroughfares off it. Probably Salonika will never quite know those days again.

If there is one unforgettable thing about the Salonika of that October 1915 it was the mud. We drilled in mud, marched in mud, ate in mud, and slept in mud not clean honest mud as one finds in the country lanes of Dorsetshire, but thick filthy mud

14

British troops in Salonika taking their daily dose of Quinine

which sucked one down to the tops of one's knee boots and entered our souls, until we longed for the day when we should turn our backs on this city of mud. That day came before we had enjoyed the doubtful hospitality of Salonika a fortnight.

One will remember the superhuman efforts of the small French force which, at this time, was gallantly carrying on the struggle up in Lower Serbia, surmounting the greatest difficulties and facing the biggest odds, in an effort to join hands with and assist the plucky Serbs. To those especially who were in touch at this time, and again later, with those undaunted Allies of ours, fighting their way hill by hill in the Serbian territory invaded by the Bulgars, their indomitable spirit will never cease to excite thoughts of admiration. The real nature of those difficulties and the odds they were contending with we did not fully realize until we shared them, nor did we realise until later how weak was the force that was so doggedly hacking its way onwards.

To the French who fought in that campaign all praise and honour, and no blame to them that the ultimate aim was not achieved. It was to assist the small force of French operating in Serbian Macedonia against the invading Bulgars that the 10th Division on the nights of October 31st and November 1st entrained for Serbia, leaving Lembet ablaze with bonfires, and Salonika sleeping the sleep of the apparently indifferent.

CHAPTER 2

The Plight of the Serbian Refugee

Ghevgeli presented a picture of a peaceful Serbian village, lifted out of the common rut by reason of the fact that a single railway line curved fantastically on the outskirts of the group of old and tumble-down houses that entitled it to a name, and ran into what was intended to be a railway station. Like the majority of Serbian villages at this time, a few old men, with a mingling of women and children, comprised its entire population, for the young and the middle-aged men and all capable of bearing arms had long ago been summoned to take their share in the defence of their country against the invader, and had left their flocks and crops to the care of the old folk and children.

One was, I think, rather inclined to take an emotional view and draw a most pitiful picture of the plight of the Serbian peasant, his country overrun by the Austro-Germans in the North, and his hereditary foe—the Bulgar—attacking him and driving him from home in the South. We who have never endured the horrors of an invasion can only draw on our imaginations for the picture of the infinitely sad and terrifying plight of a nation of refugees. To the Serbian and Macedonian peasant, however, invasion is not the life's tragedy that it would be to us. Fearful and pauperising, bringing innumerable horrors and ruination in its track, the Balkan peasant has no vague ideas of its meaning. He has suffered its horrors before and knows that he must suffer them again.

At the call of the country the young and the middle-aged, and even many of the old men, go with a stoical indifference (or can it be ignorance?) to the fact that in the life of a civilised country war and trouble is not an ever-recurring factor of life. The old men and women remain to look after the few acres of crops and the sheep until their men folk return, the cause of the unwelcome interruption having disappeared; or until, perhaps, the word comes that the hand of the invader is reaching nearer and nearer their peaceful village. Then the cattle is collected; the bags of flour are laden on the age worn bullock cart; the gaudy coverlets and garish linen so cherished in the household of the Macedonian peasant, and a few odd sticks of rudely-fashioned furniture are heaped on top.

And so, they flee. The more fortunate of the males are mounted on ponies or the most diminutive of donkeys, while the women shamble alongside, babies in arms, and so the disreputable procession struggles along the narrow mountain tracks that lead away from the invaded districts. Behind them lies their deserted village into which the invader soon marches and shows scanty respect for what the unfortunate inhabitants, now in flight, had so treasured.

When they can return to their homes, the countryside bears evidence of the ravaging hand of the invader, who has done his best, or rather his worst, during his stay. Perhaps, only a few old walls will be left standing, the crops ravaged and the fruit fields destroyed; but probably something can be done to make a living habitation out of the blackened walls, and no doubt an acre or so of crops can be found to meet the scarcely luxurious needs of the villagers.

And so, though the women wail as they trudge wearily over the mountain tracks, and the old men prattle feebly and shrug their shoulders pathetically, one has to realise that to the Balkan peasant, war and flight are events which are as certain to overtake him as death must overtake old age. The Macedonian or Balkan peasant, with the inevitable shrug of his shoulders, would tell you "It is life"—not "It is war," for Macedonia is the most ravaged country in the world, and the Macedonian peasant, often born a refugee, to a very great extent, goes through life a refugee. Their existence, particularly on the frontier, is one

19

in which trouble is the rule rather than the exception.

In Ghevgeli, the labour of gathering in the cattle, and preparations for a move, had commenced though the Bulgarians, instead of making headway in the direction of village—a very important one in consequence of the railway and one quite essential to the Allies if their progress in Southern Serbia was to continue—were being steadily pushed back and were 20-25 miles away.

The old peasants and children engaged in driving in their flocks eyed us with great curiosity as we marched through the village from the railway siding where we had detrained, singing hilariously that inquisitive Music-hall refrain—"Who were you with last night?" They were evidently wondering why the blue uniforms of the French troops who were continually passing through had suddenly given place to a strange khaki—until a typical Serbian priest, in curious flowing black robe and "flower pot" headgear, explained to the village folk that "the English had come."

On the outskirts of the village we crossed the famous swing bridge over the River Vardar, and marched through a sweltering hot day to Bogdanzi, in a field close to which we settled down under our waterproof sheets (bivouacs, unfortunately, not being available) to spend a night rendered miserable by a steady, chilling drizzle.

The following morning, we marched to the village of Causli over a first-rate Serbian Road running between two apparently endless ridges which completely domineered it. Causli, just a group of old houses which a few weeks since had been in the hands of the Bulgars, had long ago been deserted. It reposed restfully at the foot of a hill. We bivouacked on arrival in a ploughed field outside the village. It had been a long wearying march, the latter part of which had taken us over rough fields and innumerable ditches, but nothing could have been more spirited than the way our lads finished up.

Had there been anyone to witness our arrival they would have been amazed at the spectacle of a tired column of men, burdened with enormous packs, and scarcely able to drag one foot after another, gamely yelling out to the tune which will haunt every single man in the British Army till the end of his life:

We are some of the R.M.F.
We are some of the boys,
We are respected wherever we go
Oh' Oh" Oh!" Oh'" Oh'" Oh, Oh!!!!!
When we march down the avenue
Doors and windows open wide
Hear the jolly old sergeant shout
Put those pipes and woodbines out
We are some of the bhoys.

At Dedeli village on the following day, the dull roar of the French and Bulgar guns greeted us and we saw—some of us for the first time—the spectacle of Bulgar shrapnel bursting over a range of hills in the distance where the French were advancing. Beyond us we could see the villages of Robrovo and Valandova, which a few days previously had been cleared of the enemy, and to our right front, the village of Tartali, into which the Bulgar guns were sending H. E's and Shrapnel. We bivouacked on a delightfully shady spot close to the village while the French beyond us carried on the struggle for the mastery of the ridges.

There are few, of us who will ever forget Dedeli village which must have been a flourishing spot before the flight of its inhabitants. The Bulgars had fought hard for its possession, but the French, one could well imagine, had been irresistible in their advance. It had been ransacked from end to end.

Every house had its room full of cotton and outside every verandah were strings of tobacco leaves which our men eagerly seized upon as a substitute for the cigarette ration, and pronounced as extremely satisfying. There must have been at least a hundred Singer sewing machines among the litter which had been made of the contents of the houses; but what was more interesting still was the number of copies of the *Koran*, many in manuscript, which were found littered on the floors in many of the houses.

The range of hills at Dedeli, had we been on the defensive, would have afforded us a strong and well-nigh impregnable line were its flanks sufficiently strongly guarded; but we were not yet on the defensive, though the depressing news of a Serbian rout was slowly filtering through. In fact, every day it became increasingly obvious that any attempt to join hands with the stubbornly resisting Serbian Army must be doomed to failure unless strong reinforcements were forthcoming, and there seemed little hope of this possibility being realised.

Tartali was our next move. We received our orders suddenly and marched there in the dead of night by way of an apology of a road which certainly more closely resembled a steep water course. Above Tartali a battle was in progress. French troops were bustling about the village when we passed through it about 2 a.m., to settle down in a field close by. Torrential rains very quickly transferred our camping ground into a mud patch, and at daylight, when we sought out a few of the unused houses of the village as habitations, we presented the reverse of an inspiring sight.

Greatly to our disgust, no sooner had we cleaned a few houses of rubbish and suspicious litter (a polite way of suggesting a certain lively breed of "close companions!") than a French mounted messenger dashed up to the comparatively respectable residence which housed our commanding officer, and a few minutes later came the "Fall In". Still wringing wet, we paraded in the middle of the village and marched through the mud to Robrovo, where we camped in the welcome concealment of a fig plantation.

Only the day previously the French support line ran through the far end of Robrovo village, but a successful attack on the important ridge above had made the French masters of the Bulgar positions, and they were now in possession of the entire ridge domineering Robrovo and Valandova villages. Regarding it closely for the first time, we were struck with admiration for the men who had captured so formidable a position, for one could well imagine a mere handful holding it successfully against a huge attacking force.

French soldiers in Salonika, 1915

The same night found my company in the old French support line against Valandova. Excellent trenches, fashioned out of rock in many places, they ran from the Valandova Road to the summit of a high peak on the left. This peak was still fortified by French troops, to whom we made our first visit under amusing conditions.

Two other officers and myself, wishing to see exactly how our left was held, made our way into the French trenches, only to be conducted under a strong escort to M. le Capitaine. Of course, profuse apologies (and some capital French wine) were offered us when it was made clear that we were *bona fide* visitors, and we spent a most entertaining hour hearing the history of the successful operations which had carried the French so far into the invaded territory.

Just a word about the trenches we took over at Valandova. They were the most instructive relic of the last Balkan war that I saw during our 'Visit" to Serbia. Perhaps it was on account of the fact that barbed wire entanglements were rarely made use of in that war that for fully 100 yards in width in front of the entire line of tranches was a maze of holes, about 10 feet deep and from 5-6 feet in diameter.

Only with the greatest acrobatic skill was it possible to cross this diabolical "network" of traps, which had, at the time of their use, been "fixed" with a row of spikes at the bottom, and, hidden by a thin cover of grass, had effectually held up, with painful results to the attacker, attempts to capture the position from its defenders. Along the ridge marking the frontier line of Serbia and Bulgaria, was a series of formidable block houses provided with loopholes and with walls sufficiently thick to resist attack unless supported by heavy artillery.

We were, in fact, on, perhaps, the most historic battlefield in the Balkans, and evidence was not wanting of the desperate character of the battles that had been fought on this spot on the frontier. In many places the ground was littered with human bones. In one of these block houses, we established a cheerful company mess, banishing its murky atmosphere by means of huge log fires and with the aid of a large lamp which a too well laden Frenchman had been forced to leave behind him.

Valandova possessed the most fascinating little church I have come across in the Balkans. Both Bulgars and French had respected its sanctity and had been careful to leave untouched its interesting little treasures, as well as its simple but beautiful interior. With its tall white minaret, and heavy oaken doors, which opened out on to a positively fairy-like glade, it stood in the shadiest of gardens, the latter in full blossom and profuse with roses. Among the graves of peasants were those of Serbs, Turks, Bulgars and French who had fallen in battle within a mile of this most peaceful of spots, and had been laid to rest among the rose-trees under the shadow of the Church. Wandering through the village, we were given an interesting insight into the working of the French Army machine behind the firing line under conditions which called for a considerable amount of originality.

One could hardly believe that a few days previously the harassed Bulgars were bustling about these very streets, or taking cover from the shells which the French gunners were hurling into the village in preparing for the attack which ended with the enemy in flight to the ridge beyond. Valandova bustled with life. In nearly every house which could boast of four walls after the French bombardment *poilus* were pursuing their own especial task. Here were half a dozen houses resounding with the clatter and noise of forges, in another a butcher—a jaunty Frenchman with a white apron half concealing his uniform—brandishing an enormous meat chopper and hanging up his carcases for all the world like a butcher at home displaying his meat for the lure of the housewife engaged in the morning shopping.

Another group of houses was taken up by the bakery section, a most important branch, for, whatever else he goes without, except possibly his pint or two of wine, the French soldier regularly receives his loaf of bread a day under all conditions. The next house was the field post office, and then came a row of huts in which the soldier carpenters worked cheerfully over their melancholy task of fashioning neat wooden crosses and coffins out of packing cases and the doors of barns. In the centre of the village an official looking residence had been turned into an advanced hospital where a number of wounded *poilus* were lying on straw beds, tenderly cared for by the doctors who moved swiftly about among their charges. These were some of the men hit in the attack on the ridge of a day or two previously.

In one house only did we find a civilian. She was a little old lady who, the French assured us, was 105 years of age. We could quite believe it. She was dressed in the quaint garb of the Serbian peasant woman, ana we found her tottering about her one-storey house prattling feebly in a tongue we could not understand. Old age and possibly fright had robbed her of her mental faculties.

What a story of trouble and misery that old lady could have told, had it been in her power to do so, we could only imagine. The Bulgars had not disturbed her during their occupation of the village, neither had the French. She lived on the plentiful supply of rice in one of the rooms of the house. We liked to think afterwards that the end, which was then so obviously near, overtook her before that unforgettable night a few weeks later, when we passed within a mile or so of Valandova and saw it in flames, and realised that the Bulgarians were again in possession of the frontier village Peace to the old lady of Valandova.

CHAPTER 3

A Son of Serbia

It was at Valandova we made the acquaintance of our first Serbian soldier. This may seem strange but up to that time we had seen nothing of the Serbian soldiers, who were all engaged in stemming the Austro-German advance in the North and West.

Down the hillside to the spot where we had gathered to partake of the most unassuming of breakfasts, came a disreputable figure on a tired grey mare. It had been a night rendered uneasy and hideous by the noise of booming artillery, and we were not in a mood to take much interest in the unkempt, unshaved, and gaunt figure which appeared in front of us. However, the gold laced epaulettes and silver stars on his shoulder straps proclaimed him an officer of a Balkan ally, and we rose, rather reluctantly, I must confess, to give him a welcome.

He knew no English, and no French beyond the commonplace *"Bonjour, Messieurs"*, with which he accompanied his strictly correct salute.

Overhead, a shell shrieked wildly through the air, so close that the leaves of the tree under which we sat rustled.

We placed an enamel cup containing tea in front of him. He helped himself to sugar with a liberality which, in view of the scarcity of this commodity, made us nervous, and dug his knife into our one remaining tin of gooseberry jam with the air of a man feasting at a table of plenty.

Having lavishly spread the biscuit which we proffered him he started to tell us about himself in a language of sharp jerks and signs.

He was indignant when, after a great deal of trouble, we suggested the possibility of the enemy making some advance into his country, and dismissed the subject with a satisfied shrug of his lean shoulders, after explaining that there were two army corps there to impede the progress of eight of the enemy. "Ample" his shrug was intended to convey.

We enquired how he himself had fared. He pointed casually to six places, covering the whole of his body, head and legs, and with a significant gesture at each point told us how shrapnel and the enemy's bullets had practically perforated him.

He again helped himself liberally to our jam, using the only thing handy—a knife—which he proceeded in primitive fashion to thoroughly clean, without permitting a waste of this great luxury. Indeed, we imagined on one occasion that the knife had descended rather too far to be easily withdrawn!

We offered him a cigarette, though goodness only knows how it nearly broke our hearts to do so, for we were fearfully short of this luxury. Often would we cheerfully lay down the contents of our pockets for a packet of "Woodbines."

"*Ah! Bon! Bon! Anglaise* cigarette *bon! Francaise* cigarette make one" and here he coughed convulsively for the space of several minutes to illustrate to us the disastrous effect a French cigarette usually had upon his constitution.

We came to the conclusion our Balkan friend was out for what he could get, and the longing looks he directed towards us after his cigarette was finished were steadily ignored. He must have realised that all was in vain, for he produced a tin of tobacco and commenced to manufacture a scraggy weed of his own.

Conversation was becoming rather slow, so he proceeded to turn out the contents of his pockets. First, a bomb; then a locket, containing the portrait of a dapper little cavalry officer, attired in a uniform which looked as if it might have found its way from the wardrobe of the most up-to-date musical comedy company. And! Ye Gods! it was our unshaved friend, though you would'nt have believed it!

A bloodstained knife was the next article to be produced, and with this he prodded his own chest gently seven times to illustrate the number who had fallen victims, to this weapon of his.

At length, he departed. The next morning, he came again, and we, being warned in time, concealed our jam. He came, wearing the cap of a French *Zouave* soldier, and told us, indifferently, when we enquired what had become of his own, that a piece of shrapnel had come and blown it away.

If our friend was telling the truth, I sincerely hope our somewhat crude allusions to his ideas of veracity were not within his understanding. That being as it may, the following morning again saw him riding towards us, and the last we saw of him was a shrugging figure casting mournful glances at the table which we had hurriedly deserted a minute before in our dash for a place of concealment.

Where this particular Serb hailed from or what brought him unintroduced into our lines we never discovered for certain, though we had an idea at the time that his duty lay with the mob of male outcasts who every day passed along the road under a strong guard on their way to work under the French. In him we found the most perfect of misguided optimists it has ever been my lot to run against. I can still picture him regarding us sadly from a balcony in the town of Dorian a few weeks later when we marched through in the last stage of the Retreat, and his reproachful glance as he recognised us.

For once I fancy, he would have greeted us with a remark other than his customary "Bulgar finished!" had the opportunity then presented itself, for at that moment the Austro-German-Bulgar forces were rapidly closing in on the Greco-Serbian frontier town, and our dapper little Serb must have been on the point of hastily transferring himself to Greek territory unless he wished to fall into the hands of the enemy. But of that later.

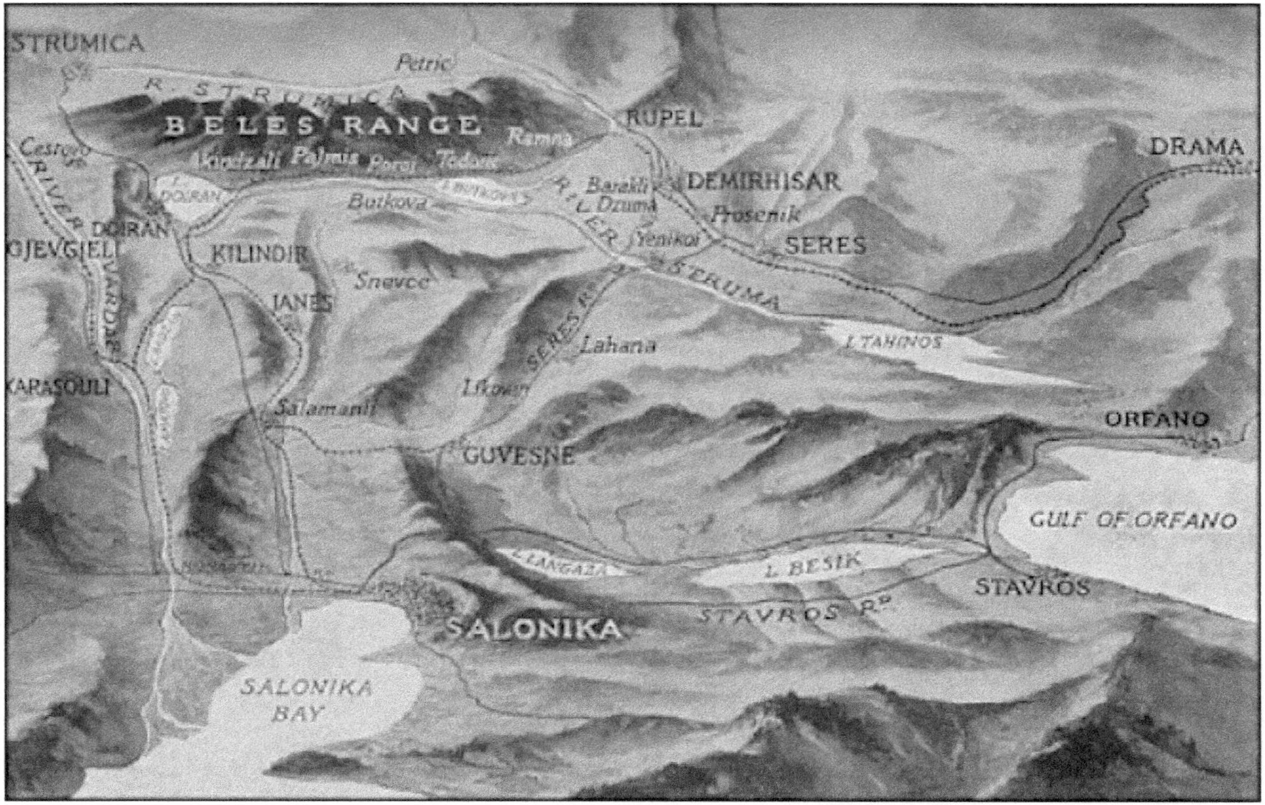
STRUMICA
Petric
R. STRUMICA
BELES RANGE
RUPEL
Cestovo
DRAMA
DEMIRHISAR
Butkova
Prosenik
DOIRAN
GJEVGJELI
KILINDIR
SERES
Snevce
STRUMA
JANES
L. TAHINOS
Lahana
KARASOULI
Salamanli
ORFANO
GUVESNE
GULF OF ORFANO
L. BESIK
STAVROS
STAVROS Rd
SALONIKA
SALONIKA BAY

CHAPTER 4

Over the Bulgarian Frontier

When the French left the ridge beyond the frontier village of Valandova and Robrovo, to push their success still further, they entered Bulgarian territory. We had been in the support line but two days when we received a hasty visit from General Bayeaux, the French general office commanding, a wonderful old soldier with the most winning of smiles, who chatted gaily with us on his way up to the ridge.

A few hours later, some French *poilus* told us in passing, "We attack at dawn tomorrow." Just before dawn on the following day, the rocky slopes were dotted with little groups of blue-coated Frenchmen, whose bayonets glistened in the early morning sunshine waiting for the word to dash over the sky line and attack the enemy entrenched on the hill beyond.

The Bulgars must have got wind of the forthcoming attack, for their shrapnel was bursting impetuously over the groups of Frenchmen who were stolidly awaiting the word to advance. At 7 a.m., the crackle of rifles and machine guns announced the beginning of the battle. In twos and threes the blue-coated figures moved over the top of the ridge, and soon hoarse triumphant cheers and terrified yells told us that the Bulgars were fleeing from the cold steel of the French and that a few acres of Bulgarian territory had been captured.

Away on the left, the attack had also resulted in success for the French. Two companies of the Foreign Legion had wrested from the enemy a high peak—the most desperately formidable position imaginable the precipitous slopes of which one would have imagined to be quite impregnable.

Two days later, I made my first close acquaintance with this peak. My company being on the left we received orders to detach a platoon to relieve the French troops holding the summit. Guided by a *poilu*, we set off through the village of Valandova just before dusk and scaled its rocky slope until after a two hours climb we reached the summit. The French commander pointed into the pitch-black night the enemy positions, and then vanished into the night with his men. It was a very relieved platoon commander who welcomed dawn the next day.

Our peak was among the clouds. From all sides it was apparently impregnable by day, and an extremely unsatisfactory objective at night for anyone endeavouring to take possession of it. Consequently we had little apprehension of an attack being attempted, especially as the French force had pushed on a fair distance on both flanks.

The summit of the peak was a maze of tremendous boulders and slabs of rocks around which a small wall had been constructed to give a certain amount of concealment to the garrison. In the comparatively few soft pieces of ground on the slopes of the peak numerous little crosses marked the resting places of both French and Bulgars who had fallen during the battle for the peak. Hundreds of Bulgar rifles and cases of ammunition and old pieces of equipment told a tale of their own. One of our first duties was to finish the burial of Bulgar bodies still lying in the open, but as we completely failed to arrive at a depth of more than a couple of feet, this was, I am afraid, a very unsatisfactory operation.

In addition to this, we speedily discovered that our intentions were misconstrued by the enemy gunners, for they lost no time in directing their guns on to us. They caught us "napping", and within a few minutes my platoon had its first casualty in the campaign. Stretchers being impossible, we placed a most cheerful "O. R." (Pte. James) in a blanket and dispatched him down the hill in the care of two comrades. With one foot shattered and a hand missing, he left us with the seraphic smile of one who knows he has earned a "Blighty one". We learnt afterwards that the journey to the foot of the peak occupied no less than 8 hours, and that when, in the French hospital at Valandova, our casualty received the tender attentions of the French surgeons it was found necessary to amputate the leg. Truly it was a "Blighty one".

During our five days' stay on the peak the Bulgar gunners spent joyful hours daily experimenting with shells against the boulders. The boulders won, and snuggling contentedly behind them, we decided that but for the starvation rations that sometimes arrived safely and sometimes did not, under cover of darkness, there were worse places in the world than "Our peak".

Nothing could have been finer or more extremely interesting than the *vista* from the peak. Away on our left we could see the River Vardar running peacefully through the picturesque Vardar valley. A single railway line followed the course of the river and ran into the Strumnitza railway station which the French had captured a few days previously and which at night time bustled like a bee hive. The Bulgar gunners had evidently marked down the railway siding, for an almost continuous rain of shrapnel was bursting over it.

But the most interesting scene of all lay in our immediate front—the Bulgarian town of Kostarino, surrounded by bright green grassy slopes, and presenting a perfect picture of snuggling contentment. Nearer still, but rather to our left, lay a couple of Bulgarian frontier block houses.

From the nearer of the two flew a Red Cross flag, and in a dip at the rear of it were a number of ominous holes where we watched the performance of a dismal task. Ever, while this was in progress, we saw a number of blue-coated Frenchmen moving cautiously towards the second block house. Immediately the air whistled with bullets and Bulgar shrapnel burst over the heads of the attackers. Three times on our first day on the peak, and at least once daily on the following days, this effort to capture the second blockhouse was repeated. It failed on every occasion. Every attempt was attended by a heavy toll on the attackers, and every night the Red Cross train steamed away from the Strumnitza siding with its load of wounded.

One morning we became aware of the fact that the French were intending an attack on Kostarino, for, below us, several companies of French troops (we learnt afterwards they belonged to our friends of the famous Legion) were massing out of sight of the enemy. It was a surprisingly easy victory, for soon after the attack started, we saw the Bulgars fleeing through the village with the French in hot pursuit. With the capture of Kostarino, the blockhouse, which had been the scene of so many fruitless attempts, must have fallen very soon afterwards.

As dusk set in the same night my platoon was relieved by another, and on the following evening, the battalion having received orders to rendezvous at Robrovo, we moved to the village of Kajali in support of the first line, which our brigade had taken over from the French.

Up to this stage we had congratulated ourselves, little knowing what we were in for, on the mildness of the Serbian winter. Occasional rain, followed by glorious sunshine, and bitterly cold nights, had so far been our experience of the Balkan winter at its worst. But now we had our first real taste of it, and I feel very sure in my own mind that none who endured it will ever seek to remind himself of those few weeks among the Serbian mountains by revisiting them after the war.

Many who had the experience in 1915 will have cause to remember it through their lives in the absence today of a limb. Frostbite worked great havoc among our men. We awoke one morning to the fact that snow lay from three to four feet on the ground, and when an intense blizzard set in to add to our troubles, we realised some of the horrors of a real Serbian winter to men so unsuitably equipped as we were in those days.

Our support trenches, fashioned in most places out of rock, gave us absolutely no protection. The village of Kajali lay a mile to our right, but might have been situated in another hemisphere for the use we could make of it. Day and night, we were exposed to the full blast of the blinding sleet and cold. I remember the arrival of the bread ration one day. It was frozen as hard as a rock. Our sole relief was found in the issue of the rum ration, but one can well imagine that we often looked in vain for

BRITISH TROOPS IN A SHALLOW TRENCH

the latter, the difficulties of transport, at all times considerable in the mountains, being now well-nigh insuperable.

All around was snow, which, caught up by the fierce wind, made the conditions decidedly uncomfortable. Our rations became increasingly short, and very soon we were faced with hardships which it was impossible to contend with. Men went down in dozens from frostbite. It was a common event to see a man suddenly fall into the snow, frozen stiff and insensible, or a man half tying, half kneeling at the entrance of the hole he had scraped for himself, quite unconscious. The battalions we were in support to suffered every whit as much as we did behind, and whenever one glanced around, one would see a thin stream of stretchers with their frozen, unconscious burdens, moving towards Kajali village, where the best houses had been turned into advanced dressing stations.

One morning when the sleet made life particularly miserable, all the men who could be spared were despatched to the village to collect what wood they could for fires, and also to dry their clothes and rid them of some of the stiffness in certain houses where fires had been got going. Unfortunately, in one tumble down house, crowded with half frozen men, the fire reached such dimensions that the building caught fire and a big part of the village was very quickly in flames. However, we derived unlimited joy from the heat given out by the blazing houses, and, consequently, most of us looked upon the mishap as a most fortunate one.

The only way to escape frostbite appeared to be to maintain a steady "double" in the snow, but, unfortunately, this invigorating exercise could not be kept up indefinitely. These days were not without their humorous side. One frequently saw men laughing uproariously at the spectacle of a frozen great coat or a blanket standing erect in the snow.

Then came—in the last week in November—the pitch-black night when our battalion moved away from the support trenches above Kajali and struggled knee deep through the snow to the front line trenches on the right of Kostarino, facing "Hill 850". An amusing incident during that journey came during the final stage, when the battalion in file, every man hanging on to the tunic of his neighbour, slid amid great merriment down the contour track which brought us to the small plateau behind the hill on which our trenches lay. We arrived just before midnight and relieved a battalion of the Dublin fusiliers, who, I believe, then went back to Tartali into so-called billets—for a rest. Our first night passed peacefully.

"Hill 850" rose some 1600 yards in front of us on a rock-strewn slope to an awe-inspiring height. On the first occasion I saw the redoubtable hill, I must confess to a grimace on over-hearing our second-in-command observe, "You will be dashing up there with the bayonet in a few days". "850" was, in fact, somewhat of a nightmare to most of us. We were separated from it by a steep-sided ravine, and a stretch of about 600 yards of snow-covered, flat country every inch of which was dominated by the hill.

I had, on the day following my first glance at it, made as intimate an acquaintance with "850" as anyone could possibly desire. Several small reconnoitring patrols had been sent out in daylight to investigate the position of affairs. My own patrol had, as its direction, "850" itself. We had crossed the ravine and the bare plateau between it and "850" without encountering any-thing more formidable than a dead Bulgar whose buttons we collected *en route* (leaving the entire contents of his pockets—soap of all things—untouched!) and arrived at the conclusion that the presence of any of the enemy on the forbidding looking "850" beyond was a myth and a delusion. A more absurd (and very nearly fatal error) I have never made.

At 11 a.m., we cautiously commenced the ascent of "850", and, in supreme ignorance of what was awaiting us, paused 1-200 yards of the summit—behind the shelter of a huge rock—to consume a leisurely lunch of bully and biscuits. Every now and again, with eyes glued to my glasses, I searched in vain for a sign of any movement above us. Lunch finished, we were taking a final scrutiny of the summit before proceeding there, when a glimpse of a bayonet, apparently showing above the parapet of a trench at the top, gave us an unpleasant shock. Judge of our surprise, when a more careful scrutiny revealed the presence of 30-40 rifles pointing from the ridge uncomfortably in the direction of our rock, and several bearded faces peering cautiously over the top down at us.

My four men, who had evidently decided that our adventure had already developed into an enjoyable picnic, very quickly disabused themselves when they realised that things might develop into something more exciting. We commenced a cautious but hurried descent, content to continue our investigation of "850" from a safer distance, and then "*Phing! Phing!*" and bullets whizzed and rifles cracked. It was clear that while we had unsuspectingly been devouring our bully and biscuits the wily Bulgar had been preparing an amiable little surprise for us, for we were fired at from our right, from where a party of Bulgars was engaged in stalking us. It certainly appeared quite miraculous that eventually, after a good many "breathers" taken in welcome hollows, we reached our own lines, for a perpetual hail of bullets followed us in our journey back from "Hill 850".

As we never, neither then, nor afterwards, made an attempt to dispute the possession of "Hill 850" with our friends the Bulgars, the results of that decidedly exciting "outing" were not apparent, but it certainly had the effect of teaching any over enthusiastic or inquisitive patrol leader, among us that no liberties could be taken during daylight with the enemy in the neighbourhood of the hill.

Chapter 5

Kostarino

I can imagine nothing so absurdly impossible as our trenches against Kostarino. Had we had a supply of dynamite we could have increased their depth to something more approaching the safety mark. A single line of wire ran along in front of the trenches about 30 yards out. So effective (?) was this that we generally made our way out, when going on patrol, through it! The trenches ran down to within a hundred yards or so of Kostarino itself. The village possessed quite the most habitable houses we had yet seen among the mountains, and looked fascinatingly peaceful in its snowy garb.

A closer acquaintance with Kostarino disclosed the unpleasant spectacle of limbs and heads protruding from the snow, for no opportunity had apparently presented itself to bury those who fell in the fighting in the village. Both British and French and Bulgar guns kept on eagle eye on the village, with the result that by day no sign of life was to be seen there and at night it was the scene of innumerable, and rather desperate little encounters between British and Bulgar patrols.

Patrolling between the ravine in front of us and the ground on the far side of it was a tri-nightly outing attended by a great deal of discomfort, but apparently very little danger, for the Bulgars left this portion of no man's land severely alone during the days preceding the great attack which marked the beginning of the end of the Serbian campaign. The snow lay several feet deep on its precipitous slopes, and a cautious commencement of the descent almost invariably ended in an undignified and hasty arrival at the bottom, followed by a breathless scramble up the opposite side.

A daring sniper here and there gave us a little trouble, and for the rest we received rather more attention than we appreciated from the Bulgar gunners. The weather was still our great enemy, and the toll it took steadily weakened our ranks. Every day saw its fresh batch of frostbite cases away to the Field Ambulance.

And a word for our position at Kostarino. I remember hearing it described as the "Neck of a bottle." No more apt description of the situation could be given, for the entire advance into the invaded territory of Serbia and into Bulgaria had been in the nature of a pin thrust. Our lines of communication appeared to the lay mind to be exceptionally flimsy. The British line was at the far end of the wedge. The fact that we were in somewhat of a dilemma must have been brought home rather forcibly to the Allied Staff when the Austro-German thrust through Serbia and the retreat of the Serbian Army made these latter operations decidedly interesting to ourselves.

An overwhelming enemy force was rapidly overrunning Serbia, and when the fall of Usbub was announced and it was obvious Monastir could only follow suit, our lines of communication were so seriously endangered that a withdrawal of the small Allied force was the only possible move which could reasonably be considered. What we did not know then was that it had some time since been decided that the Allied force should withdraw from Serbia, and that the withdrawal had been fixed to commence about this time.

It was evident that the Bulgar forces against us had received strong reinforcements, and that German guns and gunners had arrived, giving the enemy an overwhelming superiority in artillery as well as in men. It would indeed have been surprising if our insignificant force of French and British had been allowed to probe into Bulgarian territory without serious resistance for very long. We, ourselves, had no real prospect of reinforcements either in guns or men. It was obvious that the climax was about to be reached when the enemy artillery opened a bombardment on us, not only from our front, but far back on our flanks. Our own artillery was too feeble to make effective reply against the crushing superiority of the enemy's guns. Shells were unbelievably short, and the preponderance of heavy calibre guns on the other side too great.

The artillery activity was brisk on December 5th, when, scanning "Hill 850" somewhat anxiously, we were interested in a significant little group of figures calmly studying the front from the downward slopes of the hill. Our glasses revealed a party of Bulgar officers of high rank pointing significantly to certain parts of our line. We enjoyed the satisfaction of causing them to take hurried shelter after a few well directed rounds, but I think that most of us who witnessed that little incident realised that its meaning was not exactly aimed at our wellbeing!

Meanwhile, a violent bombardment was in progress some miles away almost in our rear. We were aware at this time, though only the senior officer had been "officially informed", that our positions were to be evacuated. Whether the evacuation could be made in time was a very doubtful point, for Monastir had now fallen and the large Austro-German force was undoubtedly straining every nerve to follow up its success by dealing a blow at the small Allied expedition.

On December 6th the Bulgars, urged on and strengthened by Germans and Austrians, were attacking our sadly depleted ranks in earnest along the entire British line. It was maintained with no loss of vigour and with no definite success until the morning of the 7th, when an important peak standing alone on the right of the neck of the bottle fell into enemy hands after fierce fighting, and a struggle in which superiority in numbers, following a crushing artillery bombardment, was bound to tell.

This never to be forgotten day had dawned grey, bleak and cold. The mist, which had scarcely lifted for 48 hours, enveloped us like a cloud of coal dust, blotting out even the nearest objects and hiding what was happening in No Man's Land as effectually as darkness had done. The shrill rattle of musketry went on unceasingly and the enemy gunners were playing havoc on our trenches. Our own gunners played their part as well as mortal men could under the impossible conditions. Our machines

KOSTURINO RIDGE ATTACK ON THE 10TH IRISH DIVISION

guns spat fire down into the ravine, which must soon have been crowded with enemy infantry, alive and dead. The impenetrable mist hid everything, but our toll of the attackers must have been enormous. There can be no doubt of that.

My own platoon, in a shallow trench crossing the track leading into Kostarino village, was wide awake, a report having come from the Dublins that the enemy were in the village in force. On the few occasions, however, when the mist lifted, to descend again with disconcerting suddenness, we could see no sign of them, but were rewarded for our inquisitiveness by a veritable hail of shrapnel and H. E's. While the mist played this dastardly game of lifting and lowering, we could now and again see long columns of enemy transport and reinforcements in the distance moving towards the enemy line along the Struminitza Road, but our guns had by this time become practically silent and they were allowed to continue the journey unmolested.

Evidently the enemy had given no thought to a failure of his plans. On our right, the attack was being pressed more vigorously than in our particular sector, though it never ceased here. At 3 p.m., we had to realise that part of the line had gone, for we found ourselves in the uncomfortable position of being enfiladed.

"Hold on as long as you can and then retire on Three Tree Hill", came a yell from the back of us through a hail of bullets. A few minutes later, a messenger dashed breathlessly up to our trench with the comforting (!) news that the right of the line had gone. This was perfectly obvious. An hour later—the longest hour I have ever spent—our companies in the line were ordered to withdraw, and we left with the Bulgars swarming into the trenches. We suffered casualties as we crossed the open to Three Tree Hill. It was a slow process for we had our wounded with us.

The mist, true to its previous performances in favour of the enemy, lifted and gave the Bulgar gunners and their infantry every chance of finishing us off. That we reached Three Tree Hill, where, in the shallow trench at the summit we received the most diabolical shelling; and, later, withdrew to the Kajali Ravine on orders, will always remain a miracle to most of us. The enemy pounded us with their guns unmercifully, while, from our former positions, their infantry kept up a vigorous rifle and machine gun fire on us as we withdrew.

Overhead, two Bosche planes swooped down to within a couple of hundred yards of us, directing the enemy guns and correcting their range, and at the same time adding to our discomfiture by the use of their machine guns at short range. One of our companies gave the airmen a few rounds of rapid, on which both machines quickly changed their tactics and returned to their own lines.

CARRYING THE WOUNDED

CHAPTER 6

The Retreat

There is an enormous difference between a retreat and a rout. The unkindest critic of the Anglo-French could never, by any stretch of the imagination, describe the events of December 7th to December 13th as the latter. The fact that the morning of the 8th found us little more than a mile and a half behind our old positions at Kostarino is sufficient to disabuse any idea that may exist to the contrary.

In the Kajali Ravine the roll of the battalion was taken. Across this ravine, on the hills on either side, British and French were entrenched. Our wounded were sent away, some on stretchers and some in blankets and some struggling manfully along on the arms of their comrades. Captain Bremner, our medical officer (who was rewarded with a well merited M.C.) had been back through the ravine in the darkness to make doubly sure that none had been left behind who could require mortal assistance.

As dawn broke, Lieut. Bright (who also was awarded the M.C. for bravery) came through with what remained of his platoon. During the withdrawal of the previous day, he and his platoon had rendered sterling service, and came through just before dawn after accounting for many casualties among the enemy.

The latter evidently had been taught a severe lesson, for during the night and morning there was no sign of any eagerness on his part to continue the attack. A counter attack on our part would have been a piece of useless folly, with our sadly depleted force.

The Kajali Ravine was now clear of the transport which had

filled it the day before. The loss of many brave comrades was depressing, and we learnt that, compared to other regiments, we had come off comparatively lightly. I believe the Connaught Rangers suffered the most severely, especially in the heavy bombardment which preceded the attack, and the stories of the wonderful resistance they had put up in the face of overwhelming odds on the previous day, and the fierce hand to hand struggles which had characterised it, shewed that the battalion had lived up to its splendid reputation.

December 7th was indeed a day on which the Irish as a whole showed their mettle under exceptionally trying conditions. It was a weary, hungry and almost insignificant force that kept off the combined Bulgar-Austro-German force after the severest battering, and despite the most desperate attacks hour after hour, until numbers told and the line was pierced. The day cost the enemy dearly.

The Irish fought that day with the odds at 10 to 1, for that represented the enemy's superiority in numbers.

Only those who have experienced the anxieties of a retreat under such conditions as prevailed during the winter days and nights which followed among the Serbian mountains can picture the anxious times which followed. There was no doubt the enemy had every intention of following up the initial advantage he had gained as soon as circumstances made it possible for him to do so. That, until the afternoon of the 8th, he made no attempt to do so we attributed to the fact that the punishment he had received necessitated a considerable amount of reorganisation before he could continue his effort.

At the entrance of the Kajali Ravine, a company of French troops and ourselves prepared a trap into which we vainly hoped the enemy would fall. A single French "75", in the meantime, took up a position just in our rear and played an amusing game of bluff on the enemy, who soon after midday commenced a violent assault on the French and British troops holding the hills on our right and left. Firing four shells with scarcely a break, this plucky little "75" strove manfully to convince the attackers that they had at least a battery to contend with. It would then "hitch

THE SERBIAN RETREAT, OCTOBER, 1915

up" and away to repeat the performance on another part of the line, in order to give the impression that this battery was only one of several. And so, the game continued.

The French were defending the hill on our left brilliantly while on the left ridge a company of *Zouaves* and two companies of British troops were persistently warding off a succession of attacks which were aimed at investing the new line. Every minute was of vast importance to enable the withdrawal of the Anglo-French force to proceed systematically, and we could only guess from the sounds of the battle proceeding on these two ridges how strenuously were those minutes fought for. We, ourselves, had the ravine itself in our charge, but it would have been a piece of poor strategy on the part of the enemy if he had attempted to push through with our troops still in occupation of the ridges domineering it.

At 3 p.m., the same afternoon, it seemed unlikely that the ridges could hold out much longer, and it would be our turn to stem the tide when they had gone.

Further afield, we had not the vaguest idea of how things were going with the Anglo-French. A staff officer rode up to us in the ravine to see how matters stood with us. "We and the French are giving them Hell!" he yelled to us through the din which was unmistakably growing in intensity. Our company commander smiled grimly as our cheerful informant dashed off, and remarked "I'm afraid he takes us for little children". Still, it certainly cheered us up, as it seemed that things might very well be worse than they were.

An hour later, another battalion marched on expectedly up the ravine and we found that our spell of watchfulness had ended for this day, and that it was our turn to "trek" back a few miles along the road to Doiran. Through the village of Tartali we marched by companies, pausing only a few minutes to extract a few tins of bully beef from a blazing pile of stores to keep us going until goodness only knows when. Tartali itself was in flames, and as we passed along the road just before darkness, we could see Valandova blazing in the distance. We were greeted with a fairly heavy shelling as we crossed the open country to gain the hills.

Our company set off over the mountains towards Causli village, intending to strike the main Doiran Road below the village; and as, in the pitchy blackness, we climbed up the mountain track, the Bulgars pushed home their advantage below us in the vicinity of the Kajali Ravine. It must have been a terrific fight. All of a sudden, the intense din ceased, to be followed in a few minutes by a fearful yelling, and a sky lit up by hundreds of coloured lights. The position had been carried. One might have imagined from the terrific yelling and the dazzling green, red, blue and white lights that a huge crowd was hoarsely cheering a dramatic finish to a brilliant firework display.

About midnight we arrived in the crowded village of Causli, and were allotted, I believe, the last two houses in the village for the accommodation of our company. In a room allotted to officers, there were at least 26 of us rolled up, without great coats or blankets, on the mud floor. How we slept! And imagine our surprise when, at dawn, we were informed that the sentry outside our house had attempted to rouse us during the night owing to a report that the enemy had surrounded the village. Fortunately, it proved a false alarm, for none of us had the slightest recollection of being disturbed during our slumbers.

When we turned into the Doiran Road on the following morning we received orders to proceed to the Dedeli Pass, where the companies "rendezvoused" once more, and took up a line defending the ridges commanding the road. Here we remained in a most uncomfortable blizzard for two days, and then, to our intense surprise, received orders to recross the Pass, and occupy the hill beyond Dedeli village. The enemy was carrying out his advance very cautiously. We marched back along the deserted road and found Dedeli village still garrisoned by a few cyclists. Beyond the village we took over the defence of the ridge with news that the enemy's advance guards were close up.

At 2 a.m., came sudden orders to withdraw direct to Doiran, and we left Dedeli almost as the Bulgar advanced troops marched in. There was no falling out on that march, though it was a longer one than we had done since we started our jaunt into Serbia. The retreat had almost reached its final stage and for miles we

56

passed through a deserted countryside. Men of the R.E. blew up the bridges after we had passed over them. How long would elapse before the advanced guards of the enemy would be coming along, pausing only while their engineers set to work to throw up hasty bridges in the places of those which had been blown up?

As we approached Doiran, we found that a brigade of another division had taken up the defence of the town until the withdrawal of one Division should be completed. We passed through our reliefs quite content, I confess, that we had held our last rear-guard position. We shall all, I think, retain very vivid memories of our march through the Greco-Serbian frontier town of Doiran.

Many of the shops were still open, and out on the blue lake a few fishermen were still pursuing their daily task. But the atmosphere was full of helplessness and despair. Groups of old men and women and children gazed despairingly at us as we passed, but, curiously enough, they seemed to have no idea of flight. No doubt, many had gone already, and those who remained, being faced with the choice of existing under the rule of the Bulgars for a time, on the one hand, or enduring the refugees' pitiful lot of poverty and hunger, on the other, had decided to chance the former alternative, and were prepared to trust themselves and their property to the doubtful mercy of the invader, who was now within a few miles of the town.

No wonder, that look of half frightened despair on the faces of those we left behind in Doiran! In a few hours the last of the British and French rear-guards would pass through the town; the Bulgar advanced guards would march in and the reign of the Bulgar occupation would commence. It was not a cheerful prospect, for the Serbs, better than any, know, and only too well, their Bulgar neighbours, and what to expect at the hands of a Bulgarian Army flushed with the conquest of this last little piece of Serbian territory.

Ambulances were removing the last batch of sick and wounded from the church over which flew the Red Cross as we halted for a rest at the far end of the town.

Between Doiran town and the railway station, we passed the Greek frontier guards, and wondered if the pursuing Bulgars would cry a "Halt" on reaching the Greek frontier.

What a scene the Railway Station and the vicinity presented! A maze of transport and encamped battalions already preparing to move off; *Poilus* driving flocks of sheep before them; refugees with their disreputable belongings laden on aged bullock carts and going goodness only knew where! We camped about a mile from the Station, and the same night we left Doiran in a goods train. The Bulgar guns were bombarding the town as we left.

Our train steamed laboriously into Salonika a few hours after dawn on the 13th—and, for us, the curtain descended on the first act of the Balkan drama.

What a feast there was awaiting us near the railway platform at which we alighted. Steaming hot tea, the best army biscuits (not the Spratt's dog brand!) and as much cheese as we could do with, with that rarest of all things, a genial human D.A.Q.M.G., bustling about urging our hungry little band to eat their fill. How we ate!

As we trudged along to our camp a few miles outside the city we passed what remained of a Serbian Battalion marching in. It was the most tragic picture I have ever seen. Dirty, torn and ragged, they shambled along, and one could only guess the hardships and sufferings through which they had gone.

A few days later we read with rather considerable amusement the triumphant manifesto of King Ferdinand of Bulgaria. So, we had been annihilated! With Mark Twain, we might reasonably have observed that this was an exaggeration (to say the least of it), for though rather weak, and admittedly somewhat tired, the Tenth Division was still very much "alive and kicking."

SALONIKA FRONT—TRANSPORT ON THE ROAD

Letter 1: In Greek Macedonia

The Balkans, August 17th, 1916.

My dear Teddie,

Can you imagine anything more uninspiring than digging trenches, constructing roads (for the Greeks who should make them themselves) and breaking stones? I ask this seriously for therein lies my plea for pardon for my apparent flagrant neglect of you for months past. I am sure you will agree there is nothing.

You ask me how the war is going on in our part of the world. My dear chap, it isn't going on. But we have dug a really beautiful line and have become absolutely the last word in soldiers in case one side or the other should suddenly decide that it's time it does go on! I shouldn't care to hazard a guess as to how far we are away from our old foe the Bulgar, but it is certainly sufficiently far to leave us nicely undisturbed and peaceful at nights.

To be candid, old chap, these are times when most of us curse energetically and vigorously because an unkind fate has apparently decided that we shall mark time in this delightful(?) Macedonia for the rest of our lives. I wonder! Today the first ray of hope for many months has appeared. But of this later.

I think I told you, as fully as an unscrupulous censor would allow, the story of our jaunt into the "wilds" of Serbia last year, so I will now start to bore you with just a few facts regarding our unadventurous life since then.

Salonika itself has scarcely seen us. We had just a couple of days encamped outside the city on our return, and then you might have seen us trudging along the rough mountain tracks—now, my dear Teddie, beautiful light grey winding roads towards

61

the plains in which lie the Lakes of Langaza and Beshik. One of the prettiest views imaginable presented itself as we commenced the downward slope to the plains, and the blue waters of Langaza Lake came into view.

The white minarets of the town of Langaza peep out among the trees which surround it, and, close by, the old Roman tower of Avasil cast its shade on the lake beyond, presenting a picture worthy of Venice.

Well, old man, it was on the foothills overlooking the twin lakes that we spent endless days digging, digging and digging, against the time when an enterprising foe should sweep down on us over the Struma and cross the mountains with the idea of the pushing us into the sea. But, as you know, he didn't! So, after we had constructed our formidable defences, and had torn our fingers placing miles of barbed wire in front of them, we marched off and made roads for the benefit of the Greek Nation.

The Macedonian mosquito, meanwhile, was engaged in doing his worst, with much success; sending us off to hospital in hundreds for a "rest", and, alas! some of us for a rest from which there is no return. I am going to skip over these months in fever-stricken Macedonia, of hot scorching days which reminded me very much of those fine old pre-war days we spent on adjoining "Totums" in the low country of "Ceylon" down "Kurunegalle way." And; by the way, old chap, Kurunegalle is a health resort compared to this God-forsaken land during the hot months.

Today finds us at Kamara, a small Macedonian village which snuggles in a valley about 15 miles North of Salonika, on the far side of the famous Derbend Pass. And I may as well tell you great rumours are afloat, for tomorrow we were to have started brigade manoeuvres and news has just come through that they are cancelled.

More than that, we are ordered to be ready to move tomorrow night. Rumour hath it that we march to Kilindir, in the vicinity of which the French are entrenched, and from which direction the distant thunder of big guns can even now be heard. The thought is a fascinating one, Teddie, my boy, for we have a score to wipe out with our Bulgar friends, after last December, and the sooner we have a chance of paying them out in their own coin, the better we shall be pleased.

My best *salaams* to the missis,

Yours ever, Arthur.

Letter 2: First Days on the Struma

The Balkans, August 29th, 1916.

Dear Old Chap,

Had I taken up my pencil to write to you on the day following my last, I should have said "Kilindir way it is"—for rumour looked as if she were going to belie her reputation for once. Our kits were loaded on the long-suffering mules, and our Battalion packed up and marched off towards the hills where, at night, the flashes of the guns lit up the sky. In the darkness, we pitched our camp on the slopes above Kardaza Kadi, and the following day, it being Sunday, we were to be good-boys, go to church parade and then in the cool of the evening continue our march as far as Kukus.

But in war, Teddie, as well as in love, you must count on nothing. Hardly had we turned into our hastily erected bivouacs and snuggled our pyjama-robed persons into our comfortable flea bags, when the orderly officer, in pyjamas and gun boots, rubbing his eyes and cursing his fate, the war, the enemy and life in general, dashed round turning everyone out. It was 11 p.m., and the simple telegram had come:

Prepare to move.

We flew into our clothes, for nothing less than flying will meet the case on occasions such as these—struck our bivouacs and off we went. Lights and bustle on neighbouring patches revealed that the whole brigade had received its marching orders.

But if you think we moved off along the road to Kilindir you make a mistake. We about-turned and trotted back the way we had come. Of course, there were no end of rumours, the most obvious of which—and as you will see, the true one—being that the Bulgars, who had been supposed to be still dallying at Rupel (which the Greeks had handed over without a murmur to those arch-foes of theirs), had suddenly come through the Rupel Pass and were massing at Demir Hissar. Demir Hissar, as you may know, lies almost at the mouth of the Rupel Pass on the plains. Rumour went as far as to say that the Bulgars were being held in check on the far side of the Struma River only by small detachments of French and English cavalry.

Well, to cut matters short, you had the curious spectacle of a brigade at least—I am not quite sure where the rest of the division had got to—doing a marathon race in the direction of the Struma Valley. We marched, Lord knows, how many miles each night up the Seres Road. We invariably started at 7.30 p.m. and trudged on until 5 a.m., when we disposed our tired bones on the hard ground and slept the sleep of men who had done a good night's work.

Soon, as we approached the Struma, the dull roar of guns greeted our ears, and we learnt that the enemy were in occupation of the numerous villages on the far side of the Struma, that they had cleared the small force of French out of Seres, and were kept from crossing the river by our troops whose line followed the wild curves of the river. I hear that our Yeomanry did magnificent work before retiring across the Orljak Bridge over the Struma, but, to the lay mind, it seems as if the whole thing had been a "near go" if we had meant to keep the enemy from crossing.

At Kilom 70 on the Seres Road we made our first halt for more than a day. There we had a more or less peaceful two days as escort to guns, and, incidentally saw the battery we were guarding silence a Bulgar Battery which was growing turbulent down below us on the plains. On the following day, two of our companies went into the line near Komarjan Bridge, leaving the remaining two companies back at the village of Mekes, from where I now write you. So, you see, Teddie, we have once again started "warring."

Our first casualty was Greene, a very young officer, who got a shrapnel bullet through the lungs from the first shell, I believe he, had seen. Such is luck! He was eating breakfast in the open when the enemy commenced an early morning bombardment of our position.

Back at Mekes, we have been having our own little share of excitement, for the Bulgar has developed an objectionable habit of dropping an 18-pounder shell into our bivouacs at odd moments. One, incidentally, rudely bustled our brigadier and the brigade major yesterday, while they were engaged in disentangling the knotty problems of war in the big white house by which you can identify Mekes many miles away. Needless to say, Brigade H.Q. are now elsewhere, which is fortunate, for as I write the same big white house is "getting it hot."

So here we are with a line which stretches from goodness knows where on the left to the sea on the right, with the right company of our battalion keeping a watchful eye on the tumbledown bridge which runs over the Struma at Komarjan. In Komarjan village on the far side, our friend the Bulgar lies low and must undoubtedly be having a very uncomfortable time from our guns, which scarcely ever leave him in peace.

On the right at Nigrita and Fitoki the French hold part of the line joining up with our troops on the left, while our cyclists guard the shore at Lake Tahinos and connect up with the troops which hold from the right of the lake to the sea.

Just now a daily and nightly artillery strafe is the order of things, and the big question seems to be will the enemy seriously attempt to cross the Struma in order to threaten Salonika; or are they merely there with the idea of keeping a very fair force of ours engaged, and so weaken the offensive which, to all appearances, we are about to attempt on the Dorian front or at Monistir? It is a question, Teddie, to which time alone will give an answer; but the main fact remains we are at it again after eight months of peace, and God be praised for this.

Yours ever, Arthur.

Letter 3: A day across the River

The Balkans, September 11th, 1916.

My dear Teddie,

We were just settling down to a life of comparative peace when the Signal Office messenger dashed in with an innocent message form on which was written the exciting words—

Information received states Bulgars have been ordered to attack without delay.

Well, Teddie, you would have expected that something, at any rate, would have happened even had it been only a Bulgar sniper testing his art from a tree on the other side of the river, but no. The artillery on both sides continued their monotonous bombardment, but never a Bulgar could be seen except the two bearded ruffians whom we espied day by day casting a disdainful eye about them from a sunken road where they have a strong, hidden outpost. But when another message reached us—and it was a "Priority" message, and so entitled to respect—that the French at Fitoki had espied a big Bulgar force massing on their front with the object of attacking the Fitoki ford, something, of course, had to be done.

It was the turn of another officer and myself, each with half a dozen stalwart Irishmen, for the daily patrol across the river.

Garbed in nothing more lavish than a pair of Khaki shorts and carrying our clothes on our heads, we stepped gingerly into the Struma and struggled across to the opposite bank at the un-earthly hour of 4 a.m. A couple of miles down the river another but stronger force was engaged in doing likewise, and scarcely had we dried ourselves and donned our garments when the sounds of strife on our left told us that our enterprising comrades had discovered the enemy.

The enemy was evidently under a strong impression that a general attack was imminent along the Struma front, for their gunners—both their heavies back many miles and their light artillery on the plains—opened out, shelling the river and our trenches along the banks with great vigour. Meanwhile, several Bosche aeroplanes came furiously towards the scene of action, and hovering over us seemed extremely mystified at finding that the infantry engaged in strife consisted only of a strong patrol of ours and a Bulgar post—a few hundred yards down the river bank.

We laid low until the gunners had tired of their job, and the rifles of Bulgars and British alike were being given a chance of getting cool, and then, separating, crawled on our stomachs in the direction of the sunken road where Bulgars had frequently been observed; one party of six to the left and the other (my own) to the right. Suddenly a "*phing*", and a rifle bullet whizzed past our ears.

"That's torn it," observed a man behind me.

To all appearances, Teddie, it had, for one of two things must have happened—either some idiot of a man had loosed off his rifle accidentally or a particularly keen-eyed Bulgar had espied us crawling up in his direction. In either case, bullets are not in the habit of whizzing about unless prompted by human energy, and if the Bulgars did not know that we were trespassing on their side of the Struma before, they certainly knew it now.

It is certainly rather comforting when one's orders are to reconnoitre and not to attempt to rush the enemy's out post with six men, but there we were, Teddie, with no information besides a rifle shot. So, we went on. Let me tell the rest of the story briefly.

Our two parties must have reached the sunken road almost simultaneously, about a mile apart, and found, nothing! We both trespassed further afield when a "hailstorm" started. It also hailed over on the left where the other party had disappeared. Every tree seemed to be spitting forth fire; every little bank seemed to be concealing a Manlicher belching forth rapid fire.

Need I say, Teddie, that we returned to that sunken road without undue delay. Even the sunken road, however, was in full view of the enemy, for the firing never ceased, and little spurts dug up the earth all around us. You can imagine my relief then when, away in the distance, I discerned the heads of the other party passing rapidly through a maize field in the direction of the river, and realised that having discovered the enemy's outpost line they were, according to our orders, making their way back as best they could; especially when, with a yelling such as we had not heard since Serbia, a mob of disreputable looking ruffians turned a bend in the sunken road and came for us at full gallop.

Well, old chap, had we been heroes we would, I suppose, have remained where we were, regarding with the greatest *sang froid* the little spurts of earth flying up around us and having set ourselves to the task of polishing off the odds of seven to one approaching us, then held the Bulgar outpost line, into which we had stumbled, against all comers. But, being ordinary mortals and having found out all we had desired to know, we did not. We made for the welcome concealment of a mealy field a couple of hundred yards away, and there awaited the following up of the enemy. But the Bulgar had done his work, had held his outpost against the attack of an enemy raiding party of 6 and was satisfied. We saw him no more.

I will not weary you with the account of the numerous jaunts across the river, except to say that in the case of two other patrols of ours which tested this Bulgar sunken road, a similar welcome to ours awaited them. Further down the river an attack in force taught the enemy a sharp lesson, and it was a glorious sightseeing our artillery at work on a force of Bulgars in full flight after our people had moved them from their position. An officer and four of our Battalion were wounded on this occasion.

You will see, Teddie, that we are having some excitement from all this, though you will understand what I mean when I tell you that we want to get on with the real thing and see the end of these nibblings.

The heat in this precious country is something awful still, but they say the winter will be on us soon. My best *salaams*,

Yours ever, Arthur.

Letter 4: Annoying the Bulgars

The Balkans, September 28th, 1916.

My dear Teddie,

War is a humorous business, sometimes! If you know Bairns-father, you might tell him this little joke so that he can perpetuate it in picture form among his *Humours of the War*.

A few nights ago, a small listening post was sent across the Struma in the dark hours to keep watch from the opposite bank in case the enemy should attempt a surprise crossing. About 2 a.m., an officer, having waded the river up to his neck, crawled cautiously to the bush behind which the sentry was lying.

In a whisper he asked Paddy what his orders were. "Shure, Sorr, and they are nothing to sphake of," was the reply.

"Come! come!" urged the officer impatiently, "surely you can remember the orders you received."

"Well, sorr," said the sentry, "the corporal was after telling me to watch for any noises, and if I heard any noises, shurr, it wasn't any noises at all at all, but only tortoshies."

Well, old chap, we have been pursuing a policy of annoyance. One day our troops cross the river and raid Komarjan and bring back any of the enemy who fail to evince an overpowering desire to flee, or to be slaughtered, and the next day some of us go to enquire into the health of the Bulgars in Karadzakoi Bala. Needless to say, these early morning calls are not welcomed in the proper spirit; in fact, a day or two ago when we crossed the river with the usual wetting, we found Bulgar machine guns opposing us on three sides of the village, and we postponed our call. Our artillery sent our greetings over to the enemy instead, and the Bulgars having invoked reinforcements in the form of cavalry and a battalion of infantry, were forced to realise that the day went with us, for our guns laid the latter out as they scrambled for cover.

The Royal Irish Rifles have now taken over our part of the line, and here we are, back a few kilometres, "resting", which, interpreted, means a steady swinging of the pick and shovel from very nearly dawn to dusk with brief intervals of leisure when our proclivities attract the attention of the Bulgar gunners. We then snatch a few minutes grace in the welcome depths of the trenches we are digging.

A German Aviatik passed over this morning, and instead of flying high—as Bosche aeroplanes are in the habit of doing came so low that he was able to use his machine gun on us, and at the same time so surprise our anti-aircraft gunners that he got safely away after his work was done. He deserved more success with his gun, for he inflicted one casualty only—a tortoise engaged in taking an afternoon stroll!

And today we are wondering what the immediate future has in store for us, for we were to have relieved the Northumberlands in the trenches today, and this move has been cancelled. It is said that a force of the Nationalist Army of Greece has moved up the Seres road.

Optimists are again parading the ever-welcome rumours that the good old Tenth, after 16 months of active service, is at last going home for a rest. Where these extraordinary rumours originate, Teddie, goodness only knows, and it won't tell. The A.S.C. again, I fancy.

Yours ever, Arthur.

Letter 5: Driving the Enemy off the Plains

The Balkans, October 4th, 1916.

My dear Teddie,

I confess I have always indulged more or less in thoughts of envy, though quite unmixed with malice, whenever I have observed big headlines in the newspapers proclaiming to an admiring public the "magnificent conduct of British Troops" in the West or in Egypt or in Mesopotamia. Once or twice, we have had honour thrust upon us in this way—especially during the weeks we were wintering among the snow-clad mountains of Serbia and Bulgaria. And now, perhaps, Teddie, as I write, you are reading in your *Times* or *Daily Mail* that we, in Macedonia, as well as our men in France, or in the land of the Pharaohs, are doing something, at any rate, to justify our existence.

If you can, imagine a night full of bustle and a dawn rendered hideous by the thunder of scores of guns! This was the dawn of September 30th, a day which will be remembered as the occasion on which Britisher and Bulgar on the Struma Valley first came into conflict on a big scale.

Dawn found our battalion throwing up head cover in record time on the British side of the Struma, while our guns hurled their deadly missiles unceasingly into the villages of Karadzakoi Bala and Zir. And it was some bombardment! The brigade had crossed the river by Gun Bridge, and as the grey streaks of dawn appeared two battalions of this brigade were slowly advancing on Bala, which lies about a mile and a half from the river bank, a very ordinary Macedonian village, boasting the usual white church and minaret. As our gunners paved the way for the attack on Bala, the Bulgar artillery, realising that something was up, sent their shrapnel and H.E.'s whizzing over, most of them plunging into the river within a few yards of the bridge, but in no way hindering the work which was proceeding.

Suddenly, our guns became silent. There was a sharp fusillade, followed by a hoarse cheering, and we realised that the Argylls and Gloucesters had set foot in Bala. Our work now commenced, and you might have seen an unceasing stream of Khaki-clad figures laden with iron stakes, barbed wire, and bags and ammunition, running the gauntlet of the Bulgar guns as they swept the ground between Bala and the river. Bala had to be fortified against the inevitable counter attack, and we had to provide the means to do it.

Now and again a well-directed shell from the enemy found its mark, but that, of course, was only to be expected, for one cannot move in broad daylight over open country and under the very nose of enemy guns without casualties. Just then, as you will perceive, Teddie, we were filling only an unpicturesque role in the drama of the day. Meanwhile, kilted Argylls marched in the batches of prisoners who had fallen into their hands at Bala

In the second batch a Bulgar officer strode in with dignified gait at the head of the prisoners—the very picture of the re-doubtable Foxy Ferdie—a fine looking man who was in striking contrast to the disreputable mob which followed him, doffing their caps and assuring us that they were Roumanians and not Bulgars, and telling us "Bulgars finished." This, Teddie, I should mention, is the stereotyped assurance of nearly every Bulgar who comes into our hands. They told us the same in Serbia, but I flatter myself that we are not on this occasion in the least taken in. Imagine a mob of swarthy, dark-faced, bearded Balkanites, evidently very eager to gain the comparative safety of our side of the river, tearing the buttons off their dirty blue overcoats and the cheap gaudy badges off their grey caps, and pressing them on our grinning Tommies. There you have some idea of the scene.

But out beyond Bala the battle went on in grim earnest for the possession of the village of Zir, which it was evident the enemy were holding with a tenacity for which he has already gained a very fair reputation. At 3 p.m. wounded were coming in on stretchers and on their feet, and yet Zir was still in the hands of the enemy.

In Bala, the Bulgar gunners were now completing the devastating work which our own artillery had more than commenced in the early morning bombardment; while, Bulgar snipers picked out their prey from behind the advanced houses in Zir, and from points which gave them good cover along the sunken road which led from Bala to Zir. It was obvious that Zir was not going to be given up without a fierce struggle. Already an attempt by the Argylls had been held up 500 yards from the village. The Kilties had gone forward almost as soon as Bala had fallen into our hands, only to meet half way, and in the least favourable of all places, a strong Bulgar counter attack on Bala. The Argylls beat off the counter attack, but were themselves unable to go forward.

The afternoon had almost passed when orders came that Zir was to be taken forthwith. The Argylls and Gloucesters had been busy beating off counter attacks by the Bulgars, so the Royal Scots and Camerons, who had been in support during the morning, were moved up to do their share in the day's work. The Camerons were on the right, and I could not see them; but from Bala I witnessed the advance of the Royal Scots.

It was the most intensely fascinating spectacle I have ever witnessed. The Royal Scots suddenly emerged from the cover of the sunken road with bagpipes playing, and marched through a devastating fire as unconsciously as if they had been on parade. Their commanding officer led them.

As they neared the Bulgar trenches in front of Zir, the Bulgar fire suddenly grew slacker, and when the Scots were close enough to charge and dashed forward with bayonets, they found the majority of the defenders with their hands up and the remainder in full flight, demoralised by the spectacle of that cool, advancing line of steel. The Scots went through the village and pulled up on the far side, with the Bulgars either retreating in disorder or submitting to capture.

A British plane which had been ferreting out enemy nests of machine guns and snipers from a very low altitude, demonstrated its joy by "looping the loop" over the retreating Bulgars twice in quick succession, only pausing to pelt them with his machine gun at a range of little more than 100 yards. The airman them dashed back to us, and his machine wobbled alarmingly as he reached out and waved his cap to us in joyful greeting, and then doubled back to continue his task of harassing the fleeing enemy. Anything less determined than that unwavering advance of the Scots and the Camerons must have brought in its train heavy casualties to the attackers.

As it happened, the British were left masters of the situation, with extraordinarily light causalities compared to the heavy losses inflicted on the enemy. It was a memorable charge, which gave added glory to the past deeds of the Scottish Regiments, who performed it. I am going to pass over very briefly the fierce counter attacks made by the Bulgars, and the heavy shelling which attended the digging-in of the Scots. Six times the enemy advanced, determined to retake Zir, and six times they were forced back, leaving the ground strewn with their dead.

The fiercest counter attacks of all came at 2 a.m. on the following morning and again on the following night, after which the enemy was forced to realise the hopelessness of any attempt to drive the stubborn Scots back from their hard-won positions. Scottish determination and British gunnery had done their work magnificently, and the Bulgar, in his first real conflict with the British on the Struma plains, had suffered a defeat which augured badly for him in the fighting still to come.

Well, Teddie, this brings me up to that very exciting day, October 3rd, and I can assure you that it was a day which had in it sufficient excitement for the "lay soldier" to last a lifetime. Don't imagine, Teddie, that when I speak of lay soldier, I fondle any such idea that there is anything in the Tommy of the new army which reminds one of the layman, in the common meaning of the word; but as a one-time civilian myself, and one possessing the fondest hope of returning to that pleasant state of life again, I must confess that I can never quite look on our latter-day soldiers in the same light as I do the old soldiers in our midst. They stand quite alone, hard as nails, cheerful grousers at all times, the coolest in action, quite unexcited, but imbued throughout with the instinctive unforgettable fact that they are soldiers.

You must see the old soldier in action and out of action, Teddie, to realise quite what I mean when I try to describe the difference between the soldier of today, who has come up for duration, and the soldier of the old class. Together they form a combination which I think all will agree, Teddie, has really been the foundation and the real basis of the fact that our army today is one exceptionally good in quality, in addition to being a very useful one in quantity. But, to come to October 3rd.

On the previous evening, with the Bulgars still making their impetuous and very costly counter attacks on Karadzakoj Zir, without in the least disturbing the Scottish troops who held the village, we were suddenly ordered to cease work.

We knew that our turn had come, for cease work, as you will know, when there is every necessity for doing work, is not an order which is given so that one may enjoy a quiet snooze. Yenikoj—a village, lying on the left front of Zir, with the Seres Road running through its hundred or so tumble-down houses—was to be the task of our brigade.

The fact that our brigade was weaker than that at any other period, added to the report that the Bulgars were massing in force as Yenikoj or behind it, did not afford a very encouraging outlook. At 11 a.m., we were filing across Gun Bridge over the Struma, and along the sunken road which led to Zir. Outside the Scots barbed wire we lay in extended order.

At 5 a.m., hell was suddenly let loose, and our big guns sent shell after shell, into Yenikoj village. In the dim light of early dawn, one could just discern the smoke rising from the houses set alight by our artillery fire. At 5.30 a.m., the village was easily seen, and we moved up behind the artillery barrage. Two of our companies were in the right of the first wave and two of the Royal Dublin Fusiliers on our left.

Behind the leading waves came the Royal Dublin Fusiliers and a second battalion of the Royal Munster Fusiliers, the former with orders to clear the village after we had gone through, the latter to remain in support during the initial stages of the attack.

At dawn we moved forward in waves, and, much to our surprise, were allowed to reach the outskirts of the village without opposition. Here the garrison of Yenikoj opened on us with rifles and machine guns. For, perhaps, a couple of minutes we blazed back at them. And then someone yelled, "The Bulgars are running". It was enough! Our men were off through the village, charging with fixed bayonets over some half dozen almost deserted Bulgar trenches, and through at the other end. Yenikoj had fallen. As we charged, a surprising number of Bulgars emerged, and without stopping to test the quality of the force behind the lines of cold steel, commenced running like sheep.

Those who did not take to their heels waved white flags and even ran towards us, arms upstretched, preferring to be on the safe side of those advancing bayonets, which was not a surprising thing, all things considered. The majority of the garrison were fleeing for their lives, and our machine guns and rifles enjoyed a long looked for opportunity.

The first half hour in Yenikoj, Teddie, was rather curious. The fact of the matter was we had captured the village rather sooner than the big gunners had reckoned on, and we were not quite comfortable on realising that more than one of our own shells were still falling into the village. The Bulgar gunners must have been equally mystified, for they did not fire a shot. We dug in like fury when we could see no more Bulgars to slaughter, for we were quite aware that the enemy artillery would very soon wake up to the position of affairs, and that we should not have to wait long for the inevitable counter attack. We didn't.

It is curious that the Bulgar much prefers to lose a position, and then commence a series of futile attempts to retake it, than to defend it thoroughly from the beginning, for this is what he has invariably done up to the present. Nobody can deny, however, that he is a tough customer in the counter-attack.

Before long, our artillery was playing havoc among the retreating Bulgars who were now out of rifle and machine gun range. At 10.30 the first Bulgar counter attack had been stopped by our gunners, and a second was commencing. It failed to reach 1,000 yards of the village, for our artillery again got on the advancing lines and blew huge gaps in their ranks. About 2 p.m., the Bulgar batteries opened out in the most cruel fashion, while a new counter attack was launched with fresh troops. Their shelling was diabolically accurate, and we seemed to be living in a maze of H. E.s and bursting shrapnel. The telegraph poles along the Seres Road gave them the registering marks, and, of course, we suffered. The Dublins had more than their share, evidently owing to the fact that the nature of the ground left them more exposed to the shell fire than we were.

Meanwhile, the enemy infantry pushed forward for the attack with a reckless disregard for the heavy casualties they were incurring, both from the terrific barrage put up by our artillery and the machine gun and rifle fire. At 3 p.m., the enemy's bombardment suddenly ceased and the air whistled with bullets. Bulgars suddenly sprang up from everywhere. Before many of us quite realised what had happened, a mob of Bulgars had rushed up through a sunken road a little on our left and a fierce struggle ensued. It gave the enemy just a foothold at the far end of Yenikoj village.

You can imagine, Teddie, that things hummed. I am never quite certain to this day if the Bulgars seriously attempted to push home the advantage they had gained, but I know that for more than two hours a terrific fusillade was maintained and that the Irish scored. As darkness set in, we were awaiting an almost certain pressing home of the attack, but it never developed, and our Verey lights very soon revealed that as far as our own particular front was concerned the enemy had, to all appearances, given up the attempt.

A company of the Suffolks on the left of the brigade line broke up an impetuous attack by the enemy during the night.

With the exception of a few snipers who had been left behind by the Bulgars, and who were very promptly captured, a number of wounded, and a horde of dead, Yenikoj long before daylight was clear of the enemy. The Bulgar had been beaten at all points, and had retired from his footing in Yenikoj to the villages beyond, leaving the plain literally strewn with his dead.

And so, a most enervating day ended. It was a day to be remembered by us, and one, I feel sure, never to be forgotten by the Bulgars on the Struma. Never have gunners had so fine a target as that presented by the long advancing lines of Bulgars who took part in that last futile and costly attempt to capture Yenikoj from the Irish, or machine guns a better opportunity of proving their worth.

Today our barbed wire is up, and we are devoting long hours to the task of ridding the neighbouring country of the heaps of Bulgar dead. They are everywhere, in ditches, outside the houses in the far end of the village, on the Seres Road and all over the plain. It is a disagreeable task, this disposal of the carnage, but it has to be done. The still sadder one of burying our own was soon over, for the number of our dead was wonderfully small, compared to the losses in killed which had been inflicted on the enemy.

Yours ever, Arthur.

Letter 6: The Bulgar in Flight

The Balkans, November 26th, 1916.

When I wrote you last, my dear Teddie, I rather think we were just about to leave that salubrious spot—Yenikoj which a few days before we had chased the enemy out of, bringing his losses in the 3 days' fighting well up to 10,000 in killed, wounded and in prisoners. Possibly, the British casualties all told were 1,000, not more; so, you will see we scored handsomely, especially as a goodly percentage of that number will be back in the line in a few weeks, their wounds healed.

The Connaught Rangers took over from us, and we were promised a two or three days', rest after our exertions. Scarcely had we reached our extremely comfortable support line, however, and had set ourselves contemplating the joys of a full night's rest, when unexpected orders arrived by despatch rider, and midnight saw us marching up the Seres Road past the first line, outposts and everything else towards the village of Kalendra. Apparently, our cavalry had reported the Bulgars to have gone still further back after Yenikoj than we had realised.

We took up our line in the wood on the new rear side of Kalendra village and commenced making a satisfactory defensive position out of recently used gun pits and an old Bulgar trench.

The German gunners had been here, for we found several very comfortable beds and some Hun literature and newspapers dated as recently as eight days since. Our patrols soon discovered the enemy in Kalendra village, but he showed such an irresistible desire to avoid close contact with our men that the only obvious result of the first visit to the village was half a dozen chickens and several pockets full of eggs. After this there was no lack of volunteers for the village patrol!

The Bulgar really appeared to have got a bad fright these last few days on the Struma, and our cavalry even penetrated so far as Seres railway station, which lies about a mile and a half S.W. of this largest of Greek towns, and, I believe, the second one of importance in Greek Macedonia. Meanwhile, the British advanced on the left until numerous villages, which a few days before had been nests of Bulgars, were now behind our front line. This advance had one great result. It deprived the enemy of the railway cast of Seres which he had used until Yenikoj fell into our hands. Our advanced posts were on the railway embankment almost along the entire front, and Prosenik, an important town on the railway, boasting some very fine houses, to say nothing of two large churches and a school, was in our hands. The Dublins had captured it originally (with its entire garrison intact). In the hills beyond, the Bulgars were engaged in digging a regular maze of defences.

After a few comparatively uneventful days at Kalendra Wood, we were relieved, and returned to the Struma River and spent some gorgeous days there. The Struma, though dirty, gives one a capital swim, and we disported ourselves in its muddy waters every morning and evening to our hearts content. Following this we retired for a fortnight to a peaceful little village in the hills, while the division on the left pushed the enemy out of several more of their villages and captured the once flourishing town of Barakli Dzuma with its entire garrison of 380 Bulgars, at a cost of one "other rank" wounded.

Yesterday we finished another "tour" in the line, which ended with a raid on Kupri, one of the last of the now rapidly disappearing Bulgar strongholds on the plain between Demir Hissar and Seres. The Royal Irish Regiment swept through this village with great dash in the early morning and brought in some prisoners.

A most laughable development followed. The enemy evidently imagined that we had permanent designs on Kupri, and at dawn, from Posenik, we witnessed an attack in force, preceded by a violent bombardment, on the village. The Bulgars charged through with bayonets fixed, to find they had wasted a great amount of ammunition and energy on taking an undefended village.

I must tell you of one amusing incident of the first raid on Kupri. My company had been doing rear-guard to the raiders on their return, and was withdrawing along the railway embankment (the line runs through the village) when a Bulgar came dashing after us yelling "Stop Johnnie." The poor fellow had been fearfully upset at being overlooked when the Royal Irish were collecting their prisoners. His story was this:—

> I fought with the Turks against the Bulgars in the last Balkan War, and then when the Serbs captured me, I fought on their side. Then this war started. I fought with the Serbs against the Bulgars, and when the latter took me prisoner, I joined them against the British. I don't mind fighting a bit, but I can't stand those Bulgar officers."

It transpired that he was a tailor, and on the morning following his desertion he had a busy time mending the company's clothing.

Yours ever, Arthur.

Letter 7: A month in Hospital

It General Hospital, Xmas day 1916.

My dear old Chap,

The season's greeting to you and yours. I am sitting in a cosy armchair before a blazing fire, with (do you believe it?) a simply scrumptious W. and S. on a small table by my side. "What the deuce has he been up to now?" you will be asking disgustedly, with your thoughts full of war. Well, old man, I will add a white-robed and daintily-capped lady flitting softly about the room to the picture. "Hospital", you will mutter. You are right!

I have to thank for this a rather over energetic gunner officer who caused to be despatched something like 200 rounds of 60-pounder shells from his battery just over my head one night while I was escort to the guns—a pleasant cushy duty, which I usually volunteer for with suspicious eagerness!

However, on this occasion, those absurd people the artillery thought they would spend a joyful night plastering the Bulgar position, and it was soon forced upon my optimistic self that the uninterrupted sleep I had looked forward to was not going to come off. Usually, I can sleep peacefully during the most furious bombardment, but when it is carried on from a few yards in my rear I defy anyone—even a veteran such as yourself—to slumber blissfully through it. Something disconcerting had already occurred to my left ear, and, a few days later, I discovered that that confounded battery had put the finishing touch to it. A sympathetic M.O. despatched me to the field ambulance, and here I am.

The world would be lovely, Teddie, but for one thing. I have asked plaintively every day for the past month, I think, why my temperature is such an object of interest to those little tyrants of the ward. Surely, a fellow can indulge in a troublesome ear without being expected to develop a temperature!

But three times a day, with unfailing regularity, the little sister trips forward with the thermometer, and, calmly waiving aside my caustic remark that being merely a sufferer from an oper-ated-upon ear, she is scarcely likely to have the satisfaction of jotting down a triumphant "105" on my time table, leaves me to grind my teeth upon the wretched thing while she deals simi-larly with a whole crowd of other sufferers whose complaints range from a bullet in the shoulders to a broken ankle.

It always reminds me of a certain M.O., the best of good fellows, whose stock of medicines had fallen so low that only a small black bottle of "No. 9's" remained. One morning, at sick parade, five men presented themselves for treatment. One had a bad cough, and the complaints of the remainder were sore feet, a cut on the knee, a bruised head and toothache. He gave them all "No.9's", And how many men of the British Army will forget a "No. 9" during their lives? Not many, I venture to think.

Well I'm wandering, Teddie. I had intended to tell you some-thing about my journey down. You don't know the Seres Road in winter. It's terrible. It took us three days to complete the journey. At each wayside C. C. S. our motor ambulance stopped at for the might, I was put to bed protesting that my complaint needed no such drastic treatment.

It was of no avail. I was most tenderly tucked in and the hat-ed thermometer was produced. Had they been content to have taken the number of throbs in my pulse only, I should not have minded, for the majority of these gentle creatures who tend to the wants of the suffering seem to have considerable difficulty in discovering one's pulse, and, war-worn warriors that we think we are, we relish the dainty little sister who gazes with frowning brow at her watch while her fingers gently run over one's wrist in the attempt to run to earth that elusive thing—the pulse.

The day following my arrival in hospital, I passed a cheer-ful hour in the surgeon's chair, and for at least 5 days after, the fact that my temperature was regularly taken thrice daily failed to disturb me. Today for the first time my plea that the tri-daily dose of medicine is wasted on me, that my temperature is beautifully normal, and that instead of lounging in hospital I should be back amid the peaceful surroundings of the Struma, took effect on that tyrannous little nurse in whose charge I am. In consideration of the day, she has, up to the present, merely taken my pulse!

My first night in the C. C. S. I tempted providence. An old veteran soldier of 19 summers reposing in the adjoining bed, and admitted at the same time as myself, suggested during the absence of the sister that the floor would be ever so much more comfortable than a confounded bed. We accordingly rolled ourselves up in the top sheets and reposed on the tarpaulin covered floor, and slept as only men can who have hugged plain mother earth every night for months and months.

The ordeal, early the next morning, was a painful one for both of us, when our "little sister" tripped in to see how her charges were faring. Even the veteran's pathetic "It's awfully nice on the floor, sister" and the rollicking laughter of a malaria smitten 2nd Lieut. of 50 in a bed close by, failed to evoke an answering smile on the tyrant's face. And we were very meek!

Last night we indulged in a good old English romp in celebration of Xmas. We were the guests of the sisters, and I'm very much afraid, Teddie, we behaved like a pack of little school children, Matron included.

In a few days now, I shall be paying a "duty visit" to the colonel, and getting my discharge from hospital, and as long as no one ever mentions the horrible word "temperature" to me, my recollections of my month here will be very pleasant ones.

Yours always, Arthur.

Letter 8: A Policy of Inactivity

The Balkans, February 26th, 1917

My dear Teddie,

In these days of big battles and fine victories for the Allies on other fronts, our own war doings must be profoundly uninteresting. Who wants to hear that British and Bulgar patrols come into violent conflict on the Struma Plains, or that there was Artillery activity in the region of some unknown Macedonian village? I am perfectly sure you do not, and, to be candid, our daily life has been running so much in the same groove for the past few months that for the life of me I could not rouse sufficient interest in our doings lately to tell you much about them.

I haven't a single story of victory or defeat to relate to you. Our routine consists of a succession of patrols which, while they frequently develop into sharp encounters, exciting enough to us, really don't appear to be getting us any forwarder in this confounded war. And that's the rub. Here we are struck on the plains while the Bulgars languish in case on the hills above us, except for some few small outposts of theirs. The garrison of these posts I can honestly say, do not get the chance of living a life of such ease as those above them in the hills behind. We see to that.

D'ye wonder, Teddie, that one gets just a little bit fed up? When will this confounded war end? Since the first gloss of excitement wore off, I think nearly everyone must be asking this. With Horatio Bottomley we say, "In God's name get on with the war," but it seems some problem, Teddie, and I'm still waiting for the great H.B. to say how it's going to be done. It seems to me it's got to run its course. We are winning, but the Bosche and his friends are going to get their money's worth before they let us romp home the victors.

Of late, Teddie, I have detected a more or less condescending tone in your letters when referring to the share the Salonika Army is taking in this war. But I think this is rather unwarranted. I assure you we are not pursuing the pleasant life of ease that so many people appear to believe. Ask any of our men who have come to us from France, or from Mesopotamia, or anywhere you like, their opinions on life in the Balkans. You will then hear a few facts which will astonish you.

Don't imagine that I'm trying to mislead you into believing that our actual "warring" periods can be compared to the state of things in Flanders, but I fancy, Teddie, that you will agree that this is not the only point to be considered by a long chalk. Which do not prefer? A really "hot" few days, in fact, a veritable inferno of shells, trench mortars, bombs, etc, which seem to have a personal interest in yourself, and then a rest in billets; a regular mail from Blighty, the London Dailies on the day following their publication, and leave to the U.K. after fairly short periods?

Or a long drawn out month, say, in a line where one can, perhaps, cheerfully, survey the prospect in front without the danger of stopping a bullet, and then a long tramp into the mountains for a "rest" (road-making usually) for another 2 or 3 weeks, mails diabolically irregular and frequently sunk, a continual round of work day by day, and, worst of all, the very barest chance of leave to Blighty even after a year or two have passed. Added to which, during one's month in nightly reconnoitring or offensive patrols and frequent raids to keep us alive to the fact that there's a war on.

In summer, living in a malaria swamp, the effects of which follow one to the mountains during the intervals of "rest", and in winter enjoying the doubtful pleasures of the notoriously severe Balkan winter under conditions which the most cheerful optimist could scarcely call inviting?

Here, in fact, we are far out of the limelight. People ask "what on earth is the Salonika Army doing?" Well Teddie, judging from what I know of the life of our own men, and of our Allies on the Balkan front, which, as you know, is a very devil of a long one (of which the Struma valley forms but a small part), I think our W.O. communiques might say more than they do.

Perhaps, too, something might be done to disabuse the minds of these people, who, seeing a "snap" in the pictorial press of Salonika, scenes such as "footer" matches at the base, and of dug-outs around Salonika itself, fondle the impression that the Allied Army spends its time among the luring (?) attractions of the city, and that any such unpleasant factor as an enemy does not exist.

The vast majority of the men of the Salonika Army, Teddie, have never seen Salonika since the day they marched through the town on landing, and have been many miles away from this port of Macedonia since that day.

"So glad you are in Salonika and safe", is a frequent remark one finds in letters from home, and I even saw one just a few weeks ago which contained the remark—"Now that wretched Tino has gone, I suppose all fighting in Salonika will cease."

Well, Teddie, one really cannot help laughing, and the only way I can see to let people know that there is a war on out here is to let us come home on leave, for I fancy that few of our men, after enduring the Balkans all these months, would be satisfied to sit down, blissfully content to be regarded as a person who has been away on a long and pleasant picnic, while his comrades on other fronts had been at war.

Yours as ever, Arthur.

Letter 9: St. Patrick's Day 1917

The Balkans, April 2nd, 1917.

My dear Teddie,

We were holding a portion of the outpost on the Struma up to a few days ago, and even our most hardened warriors dubbed our tour as "exciting." It was in this way. Under the very nose of the Bulgar guns, which looked directly down upon us from the hills, we never have enjoyed much peace in this particularly salubrious (?) locality. Our friends across the way, in fact, frequently became annoyed with us after raids etc., and forcibly impressed upon us, by means of shells and other objectionable things, that it would be pleasant for us if we moved back a few miles, preferably, say, to the other side of the Struma River during our apparently indefinite stay in the valley.

It was on St. Patrick's Day (March 17th) that he treated us to the most furious bombardment he has been guilty of during our long acquaintance up to the present. Along the whole front he suddenly let loose his guns about mid-day, and kept going without a break, in a fashion we had hardly thought him capable of, until dusk. In our own outpost position, his bombardment achieved the stupendous result of one casualty. I confess it was more luck on our part than bad judgment on the part of the Bulgar gunners, for our redoubts were plastered to disappearing point, and the villages in the outpost line were so shattered that it was the greatest wonder in the world that a house was left standing.

As dusk set in, we had little doubt but that the Bulgars were at last going to commence their long-promised offensive, especially, as a patrol of ours, 18 in number, had only that morning encountered over 100 of the enemy advancing to take possession of the village of Prosenik, a mile in front of us.

The result of that encounter was a complete breaking up of the Bulgar force, with 25 casualties, while our own patrol (under 2nd Lieut. P. J. O'Brien, who was afterwards rewarded the M. C.) having assumed the offensive, despite the superiority of the number opposing them, suffered only 2 killed and 4 wounded, and withdrew entirely victorious after knocking out 25 of the enemy. Just before dusk however, it was reported that a force of 600 Bulgars were advancing under cover of the bombardment on Prosenik, and accordingly we sallied forth to meet them. Our gunners barraged, and when we entered Prosenik, to our surprise, the enemy cleared.

A few days later, from prisoners and deserters we learnt what possibly was the true explanation of this unusual day's happenings. King Ferdinand of Bulgaria had arrived in Demir Hissar, and, to mark the occasion, an attack in force along the whole front was ordered by the enemy staff. The bombardment was the preliminary step, and was followed just before dusk by the massing of the enemy for the attack on the British positions.

The Bulgar regiments, however, thought different, and after a half-hearted advance, finding they would meet strong opposition, and realising that this meant terrific chastisement, returned to their trenches. It seems incredible, but many things point to the possibility of this being the real explanation of the latest fiasco on the part of the enemy.

Unfortunately, on St. Pat's Day we lost one of the bravest fellows in the battalion—Pte. F. MacManamin, who had already gained the Military Medal for his bravery in the Struma fighting. The mere idea of fear never occurred to this man, who was never content unless he was at close grips with the enemy. After being wounded himself in the patrol encounter of the morning, he died practically perforated by bullets, while in the act of carrying back a wounded scout, who, with him, had been caught in the open under conditions which made the possibility of escape almost hopeless.

A Canadian by birth, he came over with the first Canadian Contingent to England. The weeks of training were too great a strain for this war eager fighter, however, and the result was he was handed his passage back to Canada and his discharge, following an incident the details of which I have forgotten. Pte MacManamin then enlisted in the Dorsets, served in France with his regiment with considerable distinction, until a Bosche bullet brought him back to England. Serbia saw him next, cheering up his comrades under the trying conditions which attended the expedition into that country in the latter part of 1915.

At the Battle of Yenikoj, on the Struma, he was a wonderful example to every man associated with him. A Bulgar sniper on one occasion was doing damaging work when MacManamin ventured forth, took the sniper in the rear, and was soon seen chasing him at the point of his bayonet into our own lines. He rescued at least three wounded men under heavy fire that day, and brought in numerous wounded Bulgars who had been left behind in the Bulgar retreat. On a further occasion, he crept up to a waiting Bulgar, pounced on him, and having felled him with a terrific blow on the jaw, pulled him up and shook hands with him and brought him in!

We laid this fearless fighter and splendid comrade to rest in the little graveyard at Yenikoj the day after St. Pat's Day, and have ever since mourned his loss. R.I.P.

Yours, Arthur.

Letter 10: Back to the Hills

July 28th, 1917

My dear Teddie,

The Macedonian mosquito, as you probably know, plays the very dickens with one during the summer months. In normal times there is no happier hunting ground for the *culex* and *anopheles* than the Struma swamps, and since the day when a few thousand unwilling Britishers came and adopted the valley as their apparently permanent place of abode, both the sprightly *culex* and the rapacious *anopheles* have been treated to such an orgy of blood lust and high living that it is fancied that in the far off days of peace, when the great unwashed population of the Struma return to their mud houses, and the last Britisher has joyfully departed, the Struma mosquito will receive such a shock of bitter disappointment (and indigestion) that his embittered soul will flee to higher regions.

This year, again, despite a lavish disposal of petrol and the feverish filling in of pools, the mosquito has held his own, and mere man, though clad in khaki, has been forced to admit defeat.

Thus, it came about a few weeks ago, that we created consternation in the minds of our bearded friend the Bulgar by clearing him out of several of his last footholds on the plain, to say nothing of the shell-shattered village of Kupri, and then unexpectedly bringing a relieved smile to his swarthy face by bodily picking up our wire entanglements and dug-out timber and forsaking the malaria swamps on the far side of the Struma. At the same time, we sent him a cordial invitation to again take up his previous abode, and even to come along to the very banks of the river should the idea take his fancy.

We now sit in joyful content here up on the hills over-looking the plain while the Bulgar pursues a blissful existence on his. Now and again patrol encounters patrol, and British and Bulgar cavalry clash down on the plains, but the Bulgars are not tempting providence by coming down in any force.

I have told you that last summer, when, with more zeal, perhaps, than wisdom, and certainly with expectations of sending our enemy at a hot pace along the road to Sofia, we sought the doubtful hospitality of the Struma plain, the Bulgar in one of the cheerful epistles discovered by one of our patrols, reminded us that "You are in the most unhealthy spot in Europe. We shall stay on our hills, and let God do the rest."

However, they did not remain there long. Now comes another bright letter from our friends.

We see you have gone back to the hills. We did the same a fortnight ago (certainly not the truth.—A). Goodbye until next September.

This afternoon, while resting in a shady spot high up, our guns suddenly disturbed the restful atmosphere, and, snatching up my glasses, I saw the somewhat interesting spectacle of a mixed Bulgar patrol of cavalry and infantry getting it hot outside one of our old villages. Presently riderless horses were dashing in all directions, and all that remained of the patrol presently emerged from the long grass—a very frightened Bulgar waving a big white flag.

But this gentleman—far from evincing a desire to present his compliments to us in person—commenced walking rapidly backwards, still waving his flag, towards his own line. This evidently annoyed our gunners, who promptly placed a shell or two in front of him and forced him to turn his footsteps in our direction, and a little later a very sulky Bulgar was being escorted up the hill by a bored British Yeoman.

Well, well, Teddie, I confess life is not so "dusty" just now. I wouldn't for the world rouse your cynical nature by adding the remark, which one man in my platoon (following a few hours jaunt down on the plain one day) made in his tri-weekly epistle to the old folks: "This is a terrible war; I wish I were in France." I don't, old chap, but when we renew the conflict and start again prodding the Bulgar, and he lets us know in a convincing way that he can prod back, perhaps I shall venture to say something equally forcible for a state of fed-upness (and who wouldn't be fed up after very nearly two years in this Godforsaken Macedonia?) prompt one to—well, shall I say, prevaricate somewhat.

I ask you, Teddie, when John Bull, hot on the trail of all slackers and evildoers caustically observes: "If you don't want to fight go to Salonika," not to fondle the idea that life out here is a continual sipping of iced lager outside Flocas, or a nightly appearance at the gay *Tour Blanche* of Salonika; for, firstly, Salonika boasts no lager beer, and, secondly, a 50 mile stroll to Salonika on a scorching Macedonian-day is not exactly encouraged by the commanding officer, or favoured by oneself in this climate.

Yours ever, Arthur.

Letter 11: Our Friend the Bulgar

Balkans, August 4th, 1917.

On St. Patrick's Day 1917, my dear Teddie, when the Bulgar artillery commenced a bombardment of our positions along the Struma Plain with unusual vigour and an intensity which left little doubt that things were going to happen, King Ferdinand of Bulgaria was reported to have arrived in Demir Hissar, that city of minarets which snuggles so cosily against the Bulgar Hills, within a mile or so of the famous Rupel Pass. No doubt His Majesty was rubbing his plump hands gleefully as he watched his gunners unmercifully pounding our lines and the villages from which, not long since, his infantry had fled at the point of British bayonets.

This was the nearest approach to an acquaintance with Ferdinand that I have enjoyed, and, this being so, I am quite ready to fall in with the popular idea that he belongs to a type that embraces all the vices from those of a greedy and grasping hypocrite to a cowardly humbug. Whenever the thought enters my head that, possibly, he possesses a few virtues among his abundant vices, I particularly like to think of the incident in Serbia when Ferdinand, on observing a forgotten Serbian post office pillar box, jumped from his car and pulled it down, stamping his feet on it with impotent rage.

But, whatever the Bulgarian *Tzar* may be, there are many who will tell you from actual experience that the Bulgar regular soldier is by no means devoid of many of those qualities which every Britisher prides himself on possessing, and generally endeavours to live up to at all times and under all conditions.

Our first impressions, formed in Serbia in 1915, were that the Bulgar was little better than an uncivilised savage, who lived for a lust of blood, and would delight in torturing his enemy for the pure joy of seeing him writhe. We heard terrible stories of the tortures inflicted on French soldiers who fell into their hands, and I have with my own eyes seen a Bulgar thrust his bayonet through an unarmed British soldier, who, cut off from his comrades, was offering to surrender.

The more we have seen of the Bulgar soldier, however, the more we have come into the way of thinking that he is not such a bad sort of fellow after all, and that he will play the game as long as his opponent plays the game too. Of the British he has no instinctive dislike. I am perfectly sure that, given the choice, individually, he would much prefer to fight with us than against us, especially after sampling the doubtful pleasures of German comradeship, during these many months of war. The Germans have done their best to instil a feeling of hatred for us in his mind, but, apparently, with not quite so much success as they desire.

It is quite the Teutonic way to tell the less cultured Bulgar that horrible treatment awaits him at the hands of the British should be fall into our hands, either voluntarily or involuntarily. One deserter, who came in, assured us that he had been told he would be eaten alive.

"That is why you came across," questioned our intelligence officer, cynically.

"I didn't believe it", replied the deserter.

In the Struma fighting throughout the Bulgar has, up to the present, revealed a sporting quality with which few people, who do not know him, would credit him. The most striking instance of this was given at the Battle of Yenikoj after a fiercely delivered counter attack had temporarily given the enemy a slight footing at the far end of the village.

Both sides were engaged in the invigorating pastime of pouring "rapid" into each other at a distance of 100 yards or so, when three of our men, observing that three wounded comrades were lying in the open between the Bulgars and ourselves, dashed over the top in order to bring them in. The Bulgar fire on the particular part of the line where this very gallant deed was being performed, immediately ceased, though it continued in every other part, with the result that the three wounded men were safely brought in to our line, and their rescuers were untouched.

It was an incident which revealed the Bulgar in a different light to that which many had previously considered him in. But this is by no means an isolated instance of the Bulgar's sporting qualities. I remember being on outpost duty at Topalova, in front of which a troop of Yeomanry were pursuing their task of keeping the Bulgar patrols in check. Several hundred yards in front lay Prosenik, a once flourishing town on the railway, which was then still in the enemy's possession.

The troop of cavalry had dismounted when an unexpected Bulgar H.E. fell among the horses, and one frightened animal dashed away in a dead line for Prosenik. A trooper promptly jumped on to his horse and galloped after the runaway. So exciting went the chase that in a few seconds our infantry were following it from their parapets, standing up in full view of any wily Bulgar sniper who might be waiting for the opportunity of an exposed head.

On dashed the runaway, the trooper still following it up, and then we realised that the Bulgar garrison of Prosenik had followed our example and were also breathlessly following the race. It was a strange spectacle—Bulgar and British standing up in full view of each other, watching a runaway horse. At length the trooper headed the animal back towards our own lines, and returned with his captive without a single shot having been fired at him.

"The Bulgar is a humorous devil," is a remark one often hears passed, and it is certain that he possesses a deal greater sense of humour than his friend the Bosche. There was rather a rage for some weeks on the part of ourselves, as well as the Bulgars, to post up (during expeditions into opposing territory) little messages for the edification of enterprising patrols on either side. I forget what the particular message was that I have in mind (they were legion), but on the day following its posting, pinned to the identical tree on which our message had been fixed, was the reply, and a *P.S.* which read:

> For goodness sake, Englishmen, write in English next time. Your French is awful.

Needless to say, we rarely racked our mental French vocabulary after this in composing our letters to the enemy.

When told in one message from us that any Bulgar who would like to look us up would be welcomed and given plenty of bread (a subtle invitation in view of the enemy's reported shortage of bread), a reply was sent to the effect that any Britisher who thought of doing likewise would be warmly welcomed, and that they had enough bread to feed all who came across, including the commandant of —— (the officer who signed our original message). The Bulgars invariably commenced their message with the prefix "Noble Englishmen", and often reproached us for having invaded their "peaceful Macedonian soil." A subtle but amusing reference to Ireland was frequently included.

But one day came a bloodcurdling message to the effect that every loyal and true Bulgar's sole ambition was to plunge his bayonet deep into the breast of the hated British, and was so unlike our hitherto cordial exchange of letters that we unanimously ascribed it to a Teutonic hand. And I fancy we were not erring.

One day, a scratch football match was in progress behind our line, and well within view and range of the enemy guns, and it certainly was somewhat surprising that not a single shell came over to interrupt our game. It was in consequence of this forbearance on the part of our friends over the way that a conscientious O.C. Company, seeking an opportunity to fill up a sleepy hour by improving the bearing of his company by an hour's drill, paraded his company in as unexposed a spot as he could find and commenced arm drill.

A shrapnel shell quickly dissipated the idea that this could be indulged in with impunity (to the delight of the whole company), and the following day a patrol discovered a message worded, as near as I can recollect—

We like to see you playing football, and we shall not shell you while you are playing football, and we are if we are going to watch you doing company drill.

One unfortunate (or fortunate) Bulgarian was brought in on one occasion with a broken leg, which our M.O. tended with the utmost care. The man merely shrugged his broad shoulders at each agonising wrench, and uttered no complaint at the terrible pain he must have been suffering. Our interpreter was informed by the poor devil that the Bulgar doctor would have unhesitatingly cut the leg off above the knee instead of saving the leg. In gratitude he tore of a tunic button and pressed it on the M.O. as a souvenir.

It was just before Barakli Dzuma fell to the British that a deserter came in and greeted the officer, to whom he was conducted, with a swarthy smile and the words, "English shelling at Barakli Dzuma very good, very nice. Me fed up."

While, on another occasion (though I cannot honestly vouch for the truth of this story), dawn revealed outside the barbed wire entanglements a Bulgar officer and his servant, the latter carrying the officer's kit and valise, being loath that his master should suffer any discomfort in his captivity.

One message I recollect—evidently of Hunnish origin, asked us why we persisted in declaring we were fighting for the liberties of small nations when we "made slaves of the Irish." This message, directed to our Irish Regiment, found its way to its destination, and, as one might imagine, evoked considerable amusement among the sons of Erin who read it.

Whenever the Bulgar succeeded in taking any British in raids or patrol encounters, he invariably let us know how his prisoners were progressing. One over-bold British patrol one night walked into a Bulgar trap and none returned to tell the tale. On the following day we discovered in our neutral letter-box a long message which ran as follows:

Noble Englishman—The privates ——and —— are wounded and are being well treated. We buried at Ko-Moroto (a village near Demir Hissar. A.) the Privates ——

100

and ———.

Come to us and we will treat you the same? The Bulgarians.

Really rather a good example of unintentional humour. We sent back a reply thanking them for the information, adding:

Have you heard about the fall of Baghdad? You should be fighting on our side.

We never received the answer to this, for the next day our "relief" was due and we went back from the outpost line for a "rest". I could relate many more instances of Bulgar sportsmanship, but those I have already told you will suffice to shew that the Bulgar, on the whole, is not a bad sort of fellow. He is a plucky fighter, but unsteady in a violent bombardment. He is seen at his best in open warfare and in a counter attack, and at his worst in the defence of a position.

Big and swarthy, and generally bearded, he is a decidedly unpleasant looking person to see coming towards you at a run with the bayonet, but one's luck must be absolutely "out" to be hit by a Bulgar bullet (unless it comes from a machine gun), for our swarthy foes are probably the worst shots among the nations at war today.

Yours, Arthur.

Letter 12: Sudden Orders

The Balkans, August 29111, 1917.

My dear Teddie,

Great doings! We have left the Struma. No! We do not know where we are going—we never do. For the moment, the fact that we have turned our backs on the hateful valley, probably never to see it again, is enough. We don't want all life's pleasures in a lump.

The order to pack up came suddenly and very unexpectedly. We had, only a few days since, finished our "rest" and were back again at our post in the new line. Down came the relieving troops, and we were soon marching off into regions which had not seen us since we came along the winding Seres Road and across the mountains, in the early spring of 1916, on our way to the fever-stricken Struma valley.

The rattle of the drums and the soft piping of the flutes reverberated over the mountains, causing white-gowned sisters to dash to the entrances of the casualty clearing stations which we passed and the A.S.C. to pause in their work of putting aside the strawberry jam in case any but the eternal marmalade should reach the front line.

The drums and fifes are playing "Brian Boru", and with a wild yell the long column of Irishmen, fill up the breach as the drums cease their rattling and the fifes their fluting for just five seconds in their exciting "*whirr*". The yell in Brian Boru is enough to waken the dead, and as the long column of khaki swings along there is no doubt that it is an Irish Battalion on the march, and a very cheerful one too.

"Where are you going?" calls out an unenthusiastic A.S.C. man.

"Blighty", comes the reply from a score of throats, at which there is much laughter, for not a man but knows that "Blighty" is not for him yet.

What great moments are these, Teddie? Marching up, or marching back—it's almost the same. The future holds for one the novelty of a change, and that is almost everything.

The prospect of new scenes and the spice of novelty give new life to the British Tommy, no matter whether he is English, Scotch, Welsh or Irish.

The last 30 miles of our journey we travelled like lords, though, I confess, we were slightly crowded and in the place of elegant motor cars we had lorries. But then one can have a real "joy ride" packed 20 in a lorry under such circumstances, and I can truthfully say that no "joy" ride of pre-war days was ever such a "joy" ride as this one. The yells that came from the long line of motor lorries as we dashed down the Seres Road were deafening. Out of each lorry gazed a sea of eager faces, excited by the first glimpse of something approaching civilization for many a month.

We came to a Salonika very different to the one we had left. Blackened walls everywhere and smoking ruins. A few days before our arrival, one of the greatest fires of all times had visited the old city, and the Salonika of old never presented such a spectacle so tragic and hopeless. The ancient Rue Ignatia which had existed through countless ages, through which St. Paul himself had passed, and had doubtless preached to the ancestors of the very Jews who had their habitations there, is now mostly in ashes. Twisted minarets appear to be on the verge of falling into the ruins around them.

Of the Rue Venezilos there is little left; the old arcade has entirely vanished. All along the sea front the scene is one of terrible desolation. It is useless to look for the Splendide, Salonika's finest hotel, or the Olymphus, who's roof garden was the great rendezvous on an afternoon, or the Odeon, the Alhambra or Botton's famous baths. Twisted tram lines and a maze of ashes are all that is left. Salonika's most palatial buildings were here, but all that remains is a heap of ruins.

Everywhere, the fire refugees are still flocking to the camps the Allies are constructing for them. It is a sad spectacle—one of the saddest I have ever witnessed. Over 60,000 people are homeless and bankrupt.

Salonika's great landmark—the White Tower—is left standing, and yesterday I had tea there following lunch at that favourite resort of Allied officers—the *Cercle Militaire* (or the French Club). At both these places, the motto is "*business as usual*" and one can forget one is in the midst of a terrific desolation.

In a few days (we hope) we shall be sailing away from Salonika for good.

Yours ever, Arthur

Letter 13: A Last Glimpse of Macedonia

H. M. Transport—September 9th, 1917.

My dear Teddie,

We have played our role in the Balkan drama. Though the curtain has not fallen our own particular part has ended.

As I write, we are ploughing our way swiftly through the smooth, sunlit waters of the Aegean. A sea of eager faces strain for a last gaze at Macedonia, perhaps the most ravaged, troubled country on God's earth. The old city of Salonika is fast disappearing from view, the still smouldering ruins presenting a pathetic spectacle. The "*Tour Blanche*", glistening white, and the numberless white minarets of the city are still discernible, and through our glasses we can make out the old decrepit walls of the ancient citadel. On our port side Mount Olymphus presents a fascinating spectacle, domineering over the green, clad marshes of the Vardar.

We had hoped to have sailed from Salonika at night, for there is no more picturesque scene than Mount Olymphus lowering in the moonlight ever the Aegean, with the twinkling lights of the city in the distance.

There is no mistaking the thrill of joy which everyone experiences at the fact that we are leaving Macedonia behind us, probably for all time. Two years have made us forget our early admiration at the inspiring spectacle of rugged mountains domineering over stretches of light green plain and beautiful lakes and curling rivers running whither they pleased and just as nature had intended them. The deadly monotony of it all had made us blind to all this long ago.

The ancient grey tower of Avise, casting its shadow on Langaza Lake, a picture worthy of Venice; the gorgeous scene from the summit of Mount Kotos from which one has a magnificent view of the Gulf of Orfano; the River Struma, from the heights behind taking its course through myriads of fruit trees; the hundreds of little villages snuggling on the mountain sides, and, in winter the effect of the sun shining on the snow-clad summit of Mount Olymphus, with the blue sea at its foot. Truly Macedonia would give anyone, but a matter, of, fact cheerful grouser of a British soldier, enough to inspire him for many months.

Well, Teddie, we loathe the country, and though most of us cheerfully accepted the invitation long ago in 1914 for a free journey to Berlin, we are not asking for a return trip to Salonika or the Balkans.

What terrific changes have taken place in this country we have just left since we marched through Salonika in October 1915, for the first time! The city has become a base for the most remarkable army of all times. Under General Sarrail, fighting shoulder to shoulder, are British, French, Italians, Russians, Serbians, Greeks and even Montenegrins. The difficulties of commanding such an army must be staggering. Against General Sarrail's troops is the bulk of King Ferdinand's Army and a strong mixed force of Austro-Germans. And how has Greece worked out her destinies?

No one has yet forgotten the maze of intrigue and hesitation which characterised the Athens Government and the former pro-German ruler of Greece for so long following the "dismissal" of M. Venizilos from power; the sensational formation of a National Government in New Greece by Venizilos, and its declaration of war on the enemies of the Allies; the startling deposition of King Constantine and the succession of Prince Alexander, and then once again the union of old and new Greece with the great patriot Venizilos back in Athens to guide the destinies of the country into the channel that honesty and wisdom should have taken her into many months ago.

Today we have a United Greece, loyal to the Allies, true to

her traditions, and ranged with them against her hereditary foe the Bulgar. The scrap of paper which bound her to help Serbia in her hour of need is no longer being ignored, for today Serbs and Greeks fight side by side, and who shall say, when war and rumours of war have ceased, that the policy of honesty and honour has not, even at the eleventh hour, saved Greece!

I wonder if you have followed M. Venizilos's career during the past two years. That he is the embodiment of patriotism I have never yet heard doubted, and no one could be sceptical on this point who realises all he has passed through and dared, in order that his country should be true to herself and the traditions of Ancient Greece. Greece possesses no man so fitted for the leadership of the nation in such times as these. I saw him at the time of King Constantine's abdication, which, as you will remember, was followed by M. Venizilos' recall to Athens to reassume the guidance of the country.

A kindly, clever face, I could quite understand the trust which the supporters of the National movement placed in him and the enthusiasm with which he was received in Athens after the ex-King Constantine's departure. There was no sign of weakness about the firm mouth, almost hidden by the grey beard, but it must have been with mingled feelings that M. Venizilos from Salonika followed the incidents attending Constantine's downfall. As a man his heart must have been torn, for no truer subject of the king would have been found than this great statesman had that king followed the best interests of his country. But M. Venizilos is a patriot before all.

Now, as we are leaving Salonika behind us, there is at least a feeling of regret at the thought of that gallant little Serbian Army still awaiting the moment when their unfortunate country is freed from the invader, and with all our hearts we wish them a speedy victory and a quick return to their native soil!

Yours ever, Arthur.

Note. After Macedonia, the Tenth (Irish) Division fought under Lord Allenby in Palestine, and was in France at the signing of the Armistice. (Author.)

LEONAUR

ALSO FROM LEONAUR
AVAILABLE IN SOFTCOVER OR HARDCOVER WITH DUST JACKET

WINGED WARFARE *by William A. Bishop*—The Experiences of a Canadian 'Ace' of the R.F.C. During the First World War.

THE STORY OF THE LAFAYETTE ESCADRILLE *by George Thenault*—A famous fighter squadron in the First World War by its commander..

R.F.C.H.Q. *by Maurice Baring*—The command & organisation of the British Air Force during the First World War in Europe.

SIXTY SQUADRON R.A.F. *by A. J. L. Scott*—On the Western Front During the First World War.

THE STRUGGLE IN THE AIR *by Charles C. Turner*—The Air War Over Europe During the First World War.

WITH THE FLYING SQUADRON *by H. Rosher*—Letters of a Pilot of the Royal Naval Air Service During the First World War.

OVER THE WEST FRONT *by "Spin" & "Contact"* —Two Accounts of British Pilots During the First World War in Europe, Short Flights With the Cloud Cavalry by "Spin" and Cavalry of the Clouds by "Contact".

SKYFIGHTERS OF FRANCE *by Henry Farré*—An account of the French War in the Air during the First World War.

THE HIGH ACES *by Laurence la Tourette Driggs*—French, American, British, Italian & Belgian pilots of the First World War 1914-18.

PLANE TALES OF THE SKIES *by Wilfred Theodore Blake*—The experiences of pilots over the Western Front during the Great War.

IN THE CLOUDS ABOVE BAGHDAD *by J. E. Tennant*—Recollections of the R. F. C. in Mesopotamia during the First World War against the Turks.

THE SPIDER WEB *by P. I. X. (Theodore Douglas Hallam)*—Royal Navy Air Service Flying Boat Operations During the First World War by a Flight Commander

EAGLES OVER THE TRENCHES *by James R. McConnell & William B. Perry*—Two First Hand Accounts of the American Escadrille at War in the Air During World War 1-Flying For France: With the American Escadrille at Verdun and Our Pilots in the Air

KNIGHTS OF THE AIR *by Bennett A. Molter*—An American Pilot's View of the Aerial War of the French Squadrons During the First World War.